RUDOLF STEINER (1861–1925) called his spiritual philosophy 'anthroposophy', meaning 'wisdom of the human being'. As a highly developed seer, he based his work on direct knowledge and perception of spiritual dimensions. He initiated a modern and universal 'science of spirit', accessible to anyone willing to exercise clear and unprejudiced thinking.

From his spiritual investigations Steiner provided suggestions for the renewal of many activities, including education (both general and special), agriculture, medicine, economics, architecture, science, philosophy, religion and the arts. Today there are thousands of schools, clinics, farms and other organizations involved in practical work based on his principles. His many published works feature his research into the spiritual nature of the human being, the evolution of the world and humanity, and methods of personal development. Steiner wrote some 30 books and delivered over 6000 lectures across Europe. In 1924 he founded the General Anthroposophical Society, which today has branches throughout the world.

CONSTITUTION OF THE SCHOOL OF SPIRITUAL SCIENCE

An Introductory Guide

RUDOLF STEINER

RUDOLF STEINER PRESS

Rudolf Steiner Press
Hillside House, The Square
Forest Row, RH18 5ES

www.rudolfsteinerpress.com

Published by Rudolf Steiner Press 2013

Previously published under the title *The Constitution of the School of Spiritual Science, Its Arrangement in Sections* in 1964; reprinted 1980

The material contained in this book is sourced from volumes 37 and 260 of the GA (*Rudolf Steiner Gesamtausgabe* or Collected Works) published by Rudolf Steiner Verlag, Dornach. This authorized selection and translation is published by permission of the Rudolf Steiner Nachlassverwaltung, Dornach

Translated by George Adams. Translations of lectures of 18 and 30 January and 3 February revised by Joan and Siegfried Rudel

A catalogue record for this book is available from the British Library

ISBN: 978 1 85584 382 0

Cover design by Morgan Creative
Printed and bound by Berforts Ltd., Herts.

CONTENTS

Dates of the lectures are given in each case and also indicate when the articles were printed for the first time in the members' supplement to the *Goetheanum Weekly*.

CONTENTS

THE ORGANIC DEVELOPMENT OF THE ANTHROPOSOPHICAL SOCIETY AND ITS FUTURE TASKS

18 January 1924   *Lecture given by Dr. Steiner at Dornach*

MY DEAR FRIENDS,

In the second number of the *Weekly News* or News Sheet—as you know, this News Sheet is called 'What is happening in the Anthroposophical Society'—you will find a communication that I have addressed to the Members; and I would like to lay special stress on the opening sentences of the article.* These sentences must be taken in all earnestness. You will allow me perhaps to read them out:

The foundation of the General Anthroposophical Society at the Christmas gathering cannot have its fulfilment in what was done or witnessed by the members who were at the Goetheanum while it lasted. Its real substance will only come into existence if in the future, everywhere, those who are devoted to Anthroposophy can feel the coming of fresh anthroposophical life as they give effect to its intentions. Otherwise the meeting would not have done what it set out to do.

There can be no doubt of it, my dear friends, the Anthroposophical Society is in need of new life. And what took place here at Christmas must be regarded as something that is not by any means finished and completed. The very least part of all that took place can be counted as complete; rather must it be that new content continually flows into this Christmas Meeting through all that happens further in the Anthroposophical Society. Hitherto one has been accustomed to regard a meeting of this kind as included within the limits set by its

* See *The Life, Nature and Cultivation of Anthroposophy. Letters to the Members,* Vol. I, p. 12.

I

beginning and its end, preserving at the most a memory of it as of an experience that is over.

Our Christmas Meeting had however a quite different character. It showed from the very beginning that it could not possibly be so regarded. We cannot look upon it as a thing that takes place and is then past and over. Its content bore a very special quality. If you look back to the Christmas Meeting, you must needs see how something which originated from the spiritual world came into being there. The attempt was made to break with all the ideas one has had hitherto of what a Society should be, and to let the spiritual illuminate and shine through every single event that took place. But as I have often said, the spiritual has its own laws. The spiritual has other laws than those that prevail in the physical world. Let us now consider what was brought into the Christmas Meeting through the fact that it had this spiritual background. Let us place it there before our minds, and then think how all the several actions and undertakings of the Anthroposophical Society relate themselves to it.

If this Christmas Meeting is taken simply in the way one has been only too ready to take earlier gatherings, then it will gradually fade away, it will gradually lose all content; and in that case it would actually have been better if we had not come together at all. For the spiritual has this property, that if it is not held fast, it disappears—not of course in the Cosmos, but for the place where it is not being pursued and fostered. What it does is to seek out other places in the Cosmos. An event such as our Christmas Meeting, my dear friends, is not to be thought of as something that takes place within the earthly realm. And so you must not imagine, if the impulse of the Christmas Meeting fails of fulfilment and is therefore wafted away and disappears, that this impulse is bound to show itself somewhere else on Earth. That is not necessary. It may seek refuge in quite other worlds.

It all comes to this. We must find the way to receive the

content of the Christmas Meeting, we must take trouble that it shall really be received. And the News Sheet for the members is to have this as its aim.

The opening number of the News Sheet will give a picture not merely of what went on at the Christmas Meeting, but a picture also of the will that lived in this Christmas Meeting. This is our particular intention in the Letters to the Members. This second number contains the first instalment, and it will be continued in the following numbers. We have had first of all to emphasise how on the one hand we have to look back to what has been in the Anthroposophical Society and then to look forward to what ought to be in the Anthroposophical Society in the future.

And it will be quite good, my dear friends, if from this point of view, we now look back a little in time, in order, as it were, to set the Christmas Meeting in its right framework. The Anthroposophical Society began in a very small way; in its early days it was included at the beginning of the century within the Theosophical Society. What was it like in those days? We may leave on one side the Theosophical Society, for what has evolved as the Anthroposophical Society has gone through its own organic process of becoming, it has come forth and unfolded from its own source, or we might say, its own seed. Those who were so to speak the original stock who formed the Anthroposophical Society were in the beginning a very small number. We met in very small circles in various places, and even the public lectures were given, to begin with, in a quite narrow setting. And it was so, that in these early beginnings no one troubled himself about the Anthroposophical Movement except those who were there in it, or took some direct part in it in one way or other. It was really, one may say, marvellously peaceful! The world took no notice of Anthroposophy. Those who gathered together in the anthroposophical circles—they alone took notice of it.

Among these were many who were able to find in the Anthroposophy that flowed forth from the spiritual world, an answer to the deepest needs of their souls. They joined in increasing numbers those circles which later became the Anthroposophical Society. Those who were not able to find a point of contact for the needs of their soul remained away, but to begin with these were simply people who were uninterested; they did not burst into anger, they simply said to themselves: 'What I find offered there is nothing to me.' And they did not come again. As long as the work went on in this way one could really work in peace and quiet, and one was in fact able within such limited circles to lead up to higher truths many who were seeking for these truths.

And it was only in an external sense that even the war brought disturbance into this earliest phase of our movement. Communication between the countries was of course no longer possible in the same way. We could not be united in intimate circles, because a terrible world-tyranny was exercised during the war. But the characteristic spiritual stream that ran and still runs through the Anthroposophical Society nevertheless remained intact.

But it is now the task of Anthroposophy not only to reach the single individual in respect of the fundamental needs of his soul, but actually to stimulate the whole of human life. Wherever the creative impulse of man is seeking for active expression from within, there this striving can find contact with the source of Anthroposophy. For Anthroposophy takes all that is *human* for its province. Thus we were able in Munich to make a beginning with an activity in the sphere of Art. And the artistic activity that found expression in the performance of the Mystery Plays brought many a member a step forward in his soul-life. He saw in pictures what he had already received by means of ideas; for ideas had hitherto been the channels into which the spiritual life had been poured.

Not even, however, did the performance of the Mystery Plays in Munich effectively disturb our peaceful path. The world really began to take notice of Anthroposophy only when the intention to build the Goetheanum began to be put into effect. Before that, there had been single instances here and there of unfriendly workings, but they had not been such as one needs to reckon with or take into account; for in the sphere of the occult the best work is done when one works positively and out of immediate impulses. When however the intention to build the Goetheanum began to take effect, when we laid the foundation-stone in 1913, something outwardly visible was placed before the eyes of the world. Now there was something for people to see, and moreover something they did not understand. From that moment the world began to take note of Anthroposophy.

In spite of the fact that even during the war we for our part still persisted in our old manner of working, the notice taken by the world at large began to grow. Students of Natural Science who had joined the Anthroposophical Movement to begin with only to satisfy the innermost and deepest needs of their soul, found that not alone were these deep needs met in Anthroposophy, but they were being led to see how every single science is coming to-day to a dead point. The sciences come to a dead point just where the true need for knowledge begins. We must have a correct picture in our minds of the state of science today. The young student studies. What he finds in his study gives him a store of information and facts. The knowledge he gains in this way has quite special and peculiar qualities. Nowhere however is it truthfully told what are the qualities of the kind of knowledge that our boys and girls have given to them at school, and in still greater measure at the Universities. The truth is, this knowledge is permeated through and through with materialistic thinking. And when today you hear on all sides the cry that materialism is finished, that science is turning again to the spiritual, it is all nothing but talk, it is a mere illusion. People talk about the Spirit, but they have not the remotest idea what the Spirit is.

The knowledge that is taught is, fundamentally speaking, nothing but a collection of materialistically conceived facts. The student receives this knowledge; but it is, so to speak, poured out over him, without his being able to orientate himself in it. The one and only orientation he can make to it is that he knows he must pass his exams. That one fact gives him, in a sense, his place in the world. But really he is strangely at a loss how to deal with the whole width and breadth of the life of science. It pours over him. He feels exactly like someone who has been caught in a regular downpour of rain. He is soaked to the skin—or rather, to speak more truly, he is thoroughly hardened by the kind of knowledge that is presented to him. One cannot say that it is worthless in itself. It is not so. Some of it is of the greatest value; but the student who has to learn it knows nothing of its value. It is imparted to him in such a way that he can know nothing whatever of its true value. Thus we may say: Present-day knowledge may be of the very highest value, but those who are obliged to receive this knowledge are never able to become conscious of its value.

Perhaps I may here be allowed to refer to a fact in my own experience that has already been mentioned—and there will be more to follow—in my autobiography (*The Course of My Life*). You will find a remarkable thing recorded there, although described in slightly different words from those I now use. It relates to the way in which I learned as a child. To speak truly, everything that came through school remained quite external to me. What I did gain through school, I gained through single personalities who made a certain impression upon me.

In the current issue of *Das Goetheanum* I have spoken of how I approached chemistry when I was at school. Chemistry today is, from a certain aspect, a marvellous thing; it commands our admiration. But presented as a science it does not hold together. The facts pour over you as if you were overtaken by a shower of rain.

Now the master who took chemistry in our school was a remarkably able chemist. He spoke extremely little. He did experiments before us, went on continually making his experiments, speaking only a few words to link on one experiment to another. This would go on for weeks together, until the time came for reports—I have not related all the more personal details—but when the time for reports was near, the pupils knew that old Gilm would now begin to ask questions.

Then one of us would summon up courage to go to him and ask: 'Herr Doktor, will the next lesson be experiments or examination?' And he would say: 'Oh, next time, I am going to examine you.' And then for two or three lessons, a thorough examination would go on.

The method itself was admirable, but it gave no possibility of really entering into the subject that was being taught. As regards the teacher himself on the other hand—his name was Hugo von Gilm, and he was a brother of the Tyrolese poet, Herman von Gilm—anyone who had a feeling for such things and had once looked into the eyes of Hugo von Gilm, would receive in this one act of looking into his eyes, more chemistry than all the facts of systematic chemistry can give; and that is saying a good deal! He had quite extraordinary eyes. They looked out into the world in such a way that you felt: He sees everything in Nature, and everything in Nature enters into him through his look. It all goes into his look, and his look rays it out again; he has it there in him. That is why we boys had the feeling that this man was related to his science differently from all the others. We called the other teachers 'Herr Professor'; he was Professor too, just as the rest of them, but we addressed him as 'Herr Doktor', because with him we felt this different relation to his science.

It was, you see, the personality that told! And from other examples I have given, you will see how it was always so. These personalities had something that for me at least was extraordinarily stimulating. And so it was that I could simply sleep through school and go in quest of the really live things for myself.

It is a fact that in the second half of the nineteenth century and in the twentieth century no one has been able to learn anything who has not himself actively made search, feeling his way step by step. Then the learning has kept pace. I must say—with a grain of salt—that I am almost surprised I was considered a good pupil; for one gets marks and reports on what one learns at school. And in school I learnt really nothing at all! Nevertheless I always counted as a good pupil.

This, then, is the point I wish to make: it is important to perceive how harmful is the manner in which the civilisation of today presents its knowledge. And a great number of scientific people who came into our Anthroposophical Society realised this, or at least felt it. They felt how the pursuit of science today comes to a dead end in each single science at the very point where the soul wants to turn what science gives into true knowledge. There is nothing in all human knowledge that can possibly be uninteresting if only it is presented in the right way. And yet how much the pupils and students of today find uninteresting!

Thus it came about that quite a number of scientific men who had come into the Anthroposophical Society wanted now to fructify the several sciences from out of Anthroposophy.

Here was an occasion for downright annoyance! Now not only was there the Goetheanum to stir them out of their lethargy, now an Anthroposophical Science was beginning to make its appearance. People saw that Anthroposophy was beginning to give things a character they did not want.

One must look at the matter intelligently and sensibly. I have often said when speaking at an anthroposophical meeting, that there are enemies going about in all our anthroposophical conferences; and it is perfectly true. One of our enemies is the fair youth of naïvety, and there is a very great deal of naïvety among our members. One or another will think he can quite easily convert some pastor or professor or doctor of medicine. It cannot be done! For in the case of most people of the present day it is not a matter of persuading and converting them in their head or their heart; the important point for them is that they stand in a certain position in life and they cannot come out of it without full consciousness of what they are doing. We have to look at the matter reasonably. How can it be possible today for many such people simply to quit the positions they hold in life? This is at the back of very much of the opposition that has arisen—nourished and kept going, of course, by all sorts of dishonourable people. As you know, hardly a week goes by without some pamphlet or other, if not a whole book, appearing against Anthroposophy.

And now, what was the result of this development? I need not enumerate here all the consequences of the Threefold Commonwealth Movement; it is enough if we deal here with the qualitative aspect of the question. But all these things, my dear friends, brought it about that the old peace and quiet that existed in the past ceased to be there, because the world began to concern itself about Anthroposophy. The result was that Anthroposophy had now to be studied and developed, not in the old peace and quiet but while it was at the same time not only being opposed but slandered and defamed. And the question arose which played so great a part in the discussions held here (in the end of November and the beginning of December) by those who had declared themselves ready to undertake the leadership of the Anthroposophical Movement. The question arose: How can we in the future cultivate Anthroposophy more strongly? The study of the essentials of Anthroposophy has been carried on continuously, in the same way as during the days of peace and quiet; nor can it really be carried on in any other way. But we are no longer living in peace and quiet. And so ways and means must be found of intensifying our anthroposophical work; that is to say, we must learn how to place Anthroposophy into the world in such a way that by virtue of its own inherent quality it cannot be hurt by the calumny of its opponents. This means that we must find a way to continue and carry further what has really been our intention with Anthroposophy from the beginning.

We have seen the results of this in the character given to the Christmas Meeting. And in truth it is essential that this Christmas Meeting should not be taken in the way that very many things have been taken in the Anthroposophical Society. A new thing must proceed from this Meeting—new, and yet only the old enlarged and extended. The Christmas Meeting has led to the fact that the constitution of the Society will contain what I have called in the second number of the News Sheet: The School of Spiritual Science.

In this connection, my dear friends, there is no denying that mistakes were made with the School of Spiritual Science at the time when the thread of the true anthroposophical life was torn and broken. I have already, in speaking of the lost Goetheanum, pointed out how little the *Hochschulkurse* (Courses on the Academic Sciences) accorded with the whole artistic style of the Goetheanum. They *contrasted* with it! And that was due to the fact that there was too strong a desire to bring into our activities the character of Schools and Universities outside. There is no need for this. We should only need it if we were able to have some sort of official recognition for our School. For the moment, what we need is the place which gives what is given nowhere else: namely, that which can guide man into the spiritual world. And that is intended to be the content, in the strictest sense of the word, of the School of Spiritual Science.

It has always been so in the schools that have guided men into the spiritual life. There was first an exoteric circle and from this one passed on to the esoteric life. The leadership of the Anthroposophical Society desires to take this fact into account, for it is a fact that lies in the very nature of Spirit-knowledge. That is to say, in the future there will be, as before, the General Anthroposophical Society, into which one may enter in accordance with the conditions described in the so-called Statutes. One will be for a certain time in the Anthroposophical Society, and will perhaps be fully satisfied with the Spirit-knowledge that is communicated in the Anthroposophical Society. Everyone should read carefully what is contained in the News Sheet already referred to; then he will feel: Yes, it is very good that in the beginning the knowledge of the Spirit is communicated to those who join; for that is the foundation for every possible path into the spiritual world.

In the first place there must of course be those who can search out this spiritual knowledge, in order that it may then be imparted. It requires however a very special Karma to possess and immediately use spiritual vision without having first carefully studied and learned of the results of spiritual research as expressed in ideas. It is nevertheless the case that generally speaking one can examine and understand what is presented as knowledge and ideas of the Spirit without having to rely on authority. It is the intention that one should in the first place, as a member of the Anthroposophical Society, pursue the study of Anthroposophy with all the consequences it entails for the several departments of life. Afterwards one should pass on to the esoteric. And the three Classes of the School of Spiritual Science which are now added to the General Anthroposophical Society will have it as their task throughout to present the esoteric aspect, varied in accordance with the different Sections as I explained these at the Christmas Meeting—but always to present the esoteric aspect.

Now there are in the Society today very many friends who have been in it for a long time. Those who join now will best be advised to remain two years in the Anthroposophical Society and only then apply for admission into the First Class of the School of Spiritual Science. This cannot of course apply to those who are, how shall I put it—the 'old boys', the 'veterans' of the Anthroposophical Society.

Hence the First Class will be started immediately, and we have announced that application should be made for it. I have indeed already received a great many applications. So that is what we have now to do: to arrange in the near future for the starting of the First Class so that the older members may also become members of the First Class. Of course we shall not be pedantic about it; mature younger members, who have a genuine and warm enthusiasm for Anthroposophy, will naturally also be able to be in the First Class. It will always be a question of inner rather than outer conditions.

We shall, however, have to fit our external arrangements to this event. I have noticed for a long time that three lectures a week, received in the way they are received, are too many. More especially recently I have observed this to be the case. There have actually been too many lectures. You must not take it amiss when I say so. Accordingly I will now begin a new arrangement. We shall make alterations from time to time, but to begin with this will be the arrangement: on Saturdays and Sundays I will speak for the Anthroposophical Society, and then every Friday I will speak for the First Class of the School of Spiritual Science.

We will thus in future have the usual membership cards for the Anthroposophical Society—these things will all be arranged as soon as possible—and we shall give out besides, membership cards for the First Class of the School of Spiritual Science. So that on Fridays will come the members of the First Class of the School of Spiritual Science, and on Saturdays and Sundays all the members of the Anthroposophical

Society. I assume of course that the members of the First Class will also appear on Saturdays and Sundays; for I want things now to be run in such a way that everyone can see: here in Dornach the Christmas Meeting is taking effect, something is coming of it.

It is now many years since I gave my first lecture on this Dornach hill—it was about the acanthus leaf*—and since that time we have been moving gradually to the point to which we have now come. The truths to which we have listened here in Dornach have been more and more esoteric. But the members who join later are thereby left in a difficult position. And I must here and now give a clear idea of what we intend to do in this matter. In future it must be possible to see in Dornach not merely *where* one arrives in the Anthroposophical Society but *how* this is done. And we shall best attain our end by continuing in the First Class on Fridays with what has been given in recent lectures up to the lecture on Sunday last; also we shall concern ourselves with inner development; in short, cultivating the esoteric in these meetings. That will be on Fridays. On Saturdays and Sundays in the near future the intention is to give an introduction to Anthroposophy. I shall not, of course, read or recapitulate the book *Theosophy* or *Knowledge of the Higher Worlds*, but I shall nevertheless endeavour to set before you the first principles, the foundations of Anthroposophy. And I assume that the goodwill to take part in anthroposophical life will not be shown by the members of the First Class saying, 'We will now go on Fridays only, for we know all the rest already'. On the contrary, I hope all the members of the First Class will be all the more interested in the ordinary lectures; for it will really be the case that those lectures will give the opportunity to receive very much of what has hitherto been somewhat neglected. So that in the future it will be possible on the one hand to see

* 7 June 1914. Lecture I in the Course entitled *Ways to a new Style in Architecture*.

here in Dornach how Anthroposophy should be studied and learned from the foundation upwards, and at the same time to receive the esoteric content of the First Class, if one has applied for admission into it and has received notification of membership.

It is important, my dear friends, that this constitution of the Anthroposophical Society, as it is now formed for the future, be understood. I hope before Sunday to find a way of working, so that we may be able to begin next Friday with the plan I propose for the three evenings. The presentation of Anthroposophy from its foundations, however, need not wait. I will begin that tomorrow.

Thus will the possibility be given to find at work here in Dornach impulses that are in unity with the Christmas Meeting. If you adopt the point of view which I have here explained, you will already be cherishing in your heart that 'more' of which we said the pursuit of Anthroposophy stands in need. Anthroposophy can neither be a theory, nor can it altogether do without the element of thought. We are living in a time when Anthroposophy would become a burning question for countless human beings on the Earth—if only the Anthroposophical Society succeeded in working in such a way that the real needs of men could 'catch fire' by what is presented to them as Anthroposophy.

The point is this . . . let me put a concrete instance before you. A wonderful 'book of life', if I may so describe it, has once again been published. It is a kind of autobiography—a description of his own life—by Henry Ford. What this 'Automobile King' places before the world as a description of his life is highly characteristic. There is something delightful and truly great about it and what he says about the spiritual and material longings of all his life, makes this impression on me: Imagine someone standing before a door. He is full of urgent needs—not exactly spiritual needs, in this instance. But what he desires is not only urgent, but justified; his voice however is quite inadequate to express his legitimate and urgent desires. He would fain cry out aloud to all the world what he desires, but his voice does not seem loud enough. So he knocks at the door, knocks urgently—invents all manner of devices to thunder out what he desires.

When I read Ford's book, I feel almost as though I myself were the door. Nevertheless, it is delightful. You feel yourself beaten black and blue in your soul, but you cherish these bruises, for the book is indescribably intelligent. And there behind that door is Anthroposophy. Hitherto, however, it has been so constituted in a Society as to make it quite impossible for that which stands before the door to come near to that which is behind it It is simply impossible. To this end we need something quite different.

Ford, after all, is a representative man. What he is on a grander scale—truly, on the grandest possible scale—is after all only representative of many, many people of our time—. The point I wish to make is this. In future we must become aware of what it is not only to be a good and studious anthroposophist. My dear friends, I beg you not to misinterpret this. It is not that I wish to make the slightest objection to those who are diligent learners of Anthroposophy. Their efforts are absolutely justified. They came into Anthroposophy; their best days were in the period when peace, and all that went with it, was prevailing, when we were spreading out quite slowly. Nothing is to be said against anyone who wants to learn. On the contrary, this must be cultivated far more intensively in the future than it has been in the years since 1918, when the attempt was made to bring all manner of academic usages and other allurements too, into the Anthroposophical Movement. But something else must now be added— which, by the way, we have always striven for. *Anthroposophy must now be represented before the world at large*, and this requires quite another *style*. This, among other things, weighed with me in deciding to take the Presidency of the Society, for thereby it will be possible for me to show to the world more fully how I should like Anthroposophy to be represented by the Society. The point of view we adopted in 1912, 1913—and that with the best intentions—was that I should withdraw into the background and only have the office of a teacher. But there came a time when this gradually proved to be impossible. My real intentions were constantly being blunted by the Society. The inner force and impulse was taken from them—especially after 1918.

Now here in Dornach, through the arrangements to which I have just drawn attention—and it is only a beginning, it will go much further—in Dornach and by the way in which Dornach works, we shall make it apparent how Anthroposophy ought to be represented and carried before the world. That will also be the best way of carrying it into the hearts of our members. Both sides will come into their own. The one which came into its own in peace and quietude will come into its own still more. And just because this side will again be cultivated rightly, in the near future, if the impulses that are going out from the leaders at the Goetheanum meet with understanding, you will see that a new possibility may thereby be discovered. There is the knocking and hammering at the door. Behind the door is Anthroposophy, but—however loud the knocking—the door has not been opened. Now at last, however, we may find the possibility for Anthroposophy herself to open the door from within. To this end, however, it *must* be made possible for anthroposophical matters to come before the world in such a way that men who grow out of the civilisation of our time with the type of mind possessed by Henry Ford, the Automobile King, will say to themselves: 'Here I have written that modern science itself is, after all, something that points to the past. Man cannot only live in the past. There must also be something that guarantees life for the future. We cannot merely absorb so much information; we must also have something that is alive. All this I have written'—(you may read this in the highly interesting book by Ford, especially in the penultimate chapter)—'all this I have written, and yet . . . something is lacking.'

And that is just where Anthroposophy belongs! It would become possible for people to speak so, if only we knew how to take in real earnest what was intended in the Christmas Foundation Meeting, so that as time went on the Christmas Foundation Meeting would not lose content but on the contrary gain more and more.

This, my dear friends, is what I wished to put before you as a kind of introduction to our future work here in Dornach.

THE SCHOOL OF SPIRITUAL SCIENCE

I

THE Anthroposophical Society—if the intentions of the Christmas gathering are carried out—will in future have to bring fulfilment as far as possible to the esoteric aspirations of its members. With this end in view, the 'School' consisting of three Classes will be established within the General Society.

It is essential that spiritual knowledge first comes before men with its results, discovered by those who know the paths to spiritual seership. To think that these results can be acknowledged only by such as are able to find them for themselves, is a prejudice. This prejudice begets another of its kind, in the idea that those who do acknowledge the results of spiritual research give themselves up to blind faith in authority. On the strength of this idea, a Society like the Anthroposophical is then declared to consist of credulous people sitting at the feet of their leaders and renouncing all independence of judgment.

But the truth is this. Just as one need not be a painter to feel the beauty of a picture, so one need not be an investigator in spiritual worlds to *understand*—within a very wide domain—what the investigator has to tell. He, by the faculties that are in him, enters consciously the worlds where spiritual Beings dwell and spiritual processes take place. He sees spiritual Beings and spiritual processes; and he sees too how the beings and processes of the physical world arise out of the spiritual.

It is then his further task to express certain domains of what is revealed to his spiritual sight in the form of ideas—ideas which no longer depend on special faculties but are accessible to the ordinary consciousness. Every man who makes them living in his soul will find that the ideas thus gained are founded in themselves. They cannot indeed be evolved out of the mere power of thought. They only come into existence when the seer expresses in them the truths revealed by his seership. But once they are there, every man can make them his own and find them well-substantiated in themselves. No one need accept them on blind faith. And if people still believe that what the spiritual investigator communicates in the form of ideas cannot be intelligible in and through itself, it is that they have blocked their own way to an understanding of it. They have grown used to feel that that alone is proved which is supported by the evidence of the senses. They have no feeling for the way in which ideas can afford mutual proof, one of another. They resemble the man who, seeing that all heavy bodies rest on the earth, believed that the earth itself in cosmic space must somewhere be supported.

Now unless it be by special destiny, no human being can come to spiritual seership without first having received in the form of ideas the results attained by seership. Except, once more, in cases of special destiny, the requisite preliminary condition for reaching seership oneself is to understand the ideas concerning that part of the spiritual world which can thus be expressed.

Here again, it is only prejudice which inspires the belief that those who have first received the picture of a spiritual world in ideal form (*Ideenform*) afterwards 'see' it by auto-suggestion. In ordinary life, when we see a person of whom until that moment we have only heard, there can be no talk of suggestion. No more can there be in this case, when the spiritual world—coming forth as it does with every attribute of reality —is perceived by the man who previously understood it in ideas.

In general, therefore, this course has to be taken: the human being first learns to know the spiritual world in

ideal form. It is in this way that Spiritual Science will be cultivated in the General Anthroposophical Society.

But there will also be those who wish to participate when
the descriptions of the spiritual world rise from the ideal
form to modes of expression borrowed from that world itself.
And there will be some who seek acquaintance with the paths
of the soul into the spiritual world in order to take these paths
themselves.

For such as these, there will be the three Classes of the
'School'. Here, in ascending stages, the work will reach a
higher and higher degree of esotericism. The 'School' will
lead its members on into the regions of the spiritual world
which cannot be revealed in ideas,—where it becomes necessary to find the means to express Imaginations, Inspirations
and Intuitions.

Here too the various departments of life—artistic, educational, ethical, etc.—will be pursued into these regions where
they receive the esoteric light and impulse to creative work.

The constitution of the 'School' and its division into
Sections will be dealt with in the next number.

27 January 1924

II

We cannot found branches of the Goetheanum at all places
where human souls are looking for Anthroposophy, for we
are a poor Society.

For those who live far away from the Goetheanum we shall
have to extend by correspondence the activities at the
Goetheanum itself, thus enabling them to take part in its
work. As to the form which this correspondence will take,
we shall have more to say in the future. It will make it possible, even for those who cannot spend a certain time at the

Goetheanum, to participate in the Classes. Such intercourse will then be supplemented by personal visits which the leaders of the Goetheanum work, or others in close touch with them, will pay wherever possible.

All this work will have to be knit together by a true anthroposophical spirit if the 'School of Spiritual Science' with its esoteric life is to prosper.

The leading workers at the Goetheanum must make it their ideal never in any way to shut themselves off from the spiritual and intellectual life of the time. They must be quick to perceive—and with the fullest interest—everything that arises in our time in the direction of true human progress.

For this reason the work will be arranged in several Sections, with an individual in charge of each. Some Sections can already be founded, and it is hoped that they will blossom out in ever-increasing activity in the future.

In a central position will be the General Anthroposophical Section. The Educational Section will for the present form a part of this, and its leadership will devolve on me. Then there will be a Medical Section, seeking to fertilise and develop the healing art with the help of Anthroposophy. Here Dr. Ita Wegman will be in charge. From time immemorial, the art of healing has been intimately, spiritually interwoven with the central tasks of human knowledge. Anthroposophy must prove its living power by re-establishing such a connection. In the 'Clinical and Therapeutic Institute' of Dr. Ita Wegman a model institution for the pursuit and practical fulfilment of this aim has been created.

The artistic life must lie very near to the heart of Anthroposophy. We have had a new thriving of artistic life for many years now, in our cultivation of Eurythmy and the arts of Declamation and Recitation*—all of which are in intimate connection with Music. There will be a special Section for

* See *Speech and Drama* (19 lectures).

this work. Frau Marie Steiner has given herself up to it in the most devoted way in the past, and the very history of the Anthroposophical Society makes her the leader of this Section of the School.

The Plastic Arts were much in evidence in the building of the Goetheanum. Around the central tasks which arose out of this work, a new style has been evolved. This, needless to say, still has to meet with many critics and opponents. At the present stage it can only imperfectly express what lies in its intentions. It will be better understood when men come nearer to Anthroposophy in general. The way in which she helped me in developing this style makes Miss Edith Maryon the leader of the Section for the Plastic Arts.

There was an old conception of *belles lettres*—or, as the German has it, *schöne Wissenschaften*—the beautiful sciences. These, in the time when they flourished, formed a bridge between Science and Scholarship as such, and the creative works of Fancy and Imagination. The idea of 'Science' which the modern world has evolved has quite eclipsed this gentler branch of learning. I shall have something to say about *belles lettres—schöne Wissenschaften*—in the *Goetheanum Weekly* in the near future. It is our good fortune in the Anthroposophical Society to have in our midst a splendid representative of these, in the person of Albert Steffen. Steffen is not only destined to be the leader of the Section for *belles lettres* but to call to life again a branch of human work which civilisation has 'shelved' to its own detriment.

Our circumstances—through the individuals who are at work among us—have also made it possible to found a Mathematical and Astronomical Section, of which Dr. Vreede will be in charge, and a Section for Natural Science under the direction of Dr. Guenther Wachsmuth. The astronomical side is particularly important to Anthroposophy, while the Section for Natural Science will show that a genuine knowledge of Nature is in no contradiction, but rather in full harmony with

Anthroposophy. By his book* which will shortly be published (*The Etheric Formative Forces in Cosmos, Earth and Man*), Dr. Wachsmuth has proved himself qualified to become the leader of this Section.

* This was followed by many other volumes in the course of Dr. Wachsmuth's life.

THE SCHOOL OF SPIRITUAL SCIENCE WITHIN THE CONSTITUTION OF THE ANTHROPOSOPHICAL SOCIETY. ITS ARRANGEMENT IN SECTIONS

30 January 1924 *Lecture given by Dr. Steiner at Dornach*

MY DEAR FRIENDS,

. . .* At this point we should really recognise what the Anthroposophical Society is intended to become. In the first place, everyone who hears of this Society should know from the very outset that it has absolutely nothing in common with any mysterious pretences. It is an absolutely public Society like any other Society.

How happy I should be if this had been understood from the very beginning, when in 1912-13 the Anthroposophical Society was instituted. For if it had been, many things would have been easier than they now are. For, you see, it was an integral part of the measure we then took, that I personally withdrew myself from the administration of the Society. I only wanted to bring into it the treasures of knowledge, the impulses that should flow into this Society. Precisely in as much as the bringer of the spiritual impulses and the official leader were not united in one person, it would easily have been possible for the Society to work in such a way as to establish in the world a true judgment of the Anthroposophical Movement.

But the Society did not work in this way, and for this reason it has now come about that I, who at the same time

* The beginning of the lecture concerning the arrangements of general lectures and Class lectures at the time is omitted here as the information is given in the four concluding paragraphs.

bring the spiritual impulses, must undertake the actual Presidency of the Society—the very thing we wished originally to avoid.

It has been an extremely difficult decision to make, for thereby in reality all things will have to become different, nor will it be very easy to make these thorough changes, after many of the habits that have crept in during these years.

In two directions above all, the Anthroposophical Society must clearly recognise its situation. In the first place it must become aware that it exists for every human being in the world, who, in his soul, is seeking for the paths to the spirit. In this respect it must be an absolutely public society—not in the least hedged-in from the outer world. In the Anthroposophical Society we must not be in the least bit narrow-minded when it comes to the admission of members.

Once this is sufficiently recognised, the presence in the Society of this or that individual who may not be altogether suited to the cause of Anthroposophy, need not occasion any difficulty. Difficulties will naturally arise, so long as you make the Anthroposophical Society responsible for every single person it contains. The Society as such should have unlimited possibilities of giving to every human being what he is looking for, in this direction.

Secondly, however, the Anthroposophical Society should realise that it has not been formed out of any vague or unknown intentions. This could and should already have been recognised in 1912-13, for at that time a considerable part of our teaching was already there, and there were also definite impulses for the physical realisation of what the spiritual world has to say to mankind in our time. It should have been understood, already then, that this Society was not founded on abstract principles, such as that this ideal or that should be adopted. . . . The Anthroposophical Society was founded on something actually in existence, namely, on the spiritual treasure that is there, that has been worked for and acquired in the long course of time. To cultivate this spiritual treasure, with all its consequences for the artistic, religious and scientific life, and to develop these consequences, is the specific task of the Anthroposophical Society. If we understand this rightly, then indeed the Anthroposophical Society differs from all other Societies in the world today, for they are not founded on existing realities, but on all manner of human intentions.

Therefore it is emphasised, in our so-called Statutes, that the Anthroposophical Society embraces those who see something right and justified in the spiritual life that proceeds from the Goetheanum. The Statutes do not say that this or that principle should be adopted. The whole thing is founded on what is—or at least, *can* already be there amongst human beings.

This is of great importance. Nay—if the Society would develop a true consciousness of the Time—it cannot do so without observing what I have now said. I beg you to take my words in deep earnestness. Our time is, once and for all, the time of great decisions. Many and overwhelming matters are being decided for mankind today. Needless to say, this 'today' will last for a long time yet, but I repeat: many and untold things are being decided for mankind today. Most people are not even aware of the extent to which this time is the time of great decisions; but in the Anthroposophical Society above all, a consciousness of this must be awakened.

This, then, on the one side: the Anthroposophical Society must not on any account set up the principle: 'Let us choose persons of confidence or guarantors, and they will decide out of their sympathies and antipathies, whom they will admit and whom they will not, as members.' This has unhappily been done, on a pretty large scale, and so it has come about that many people, when they want to enter, feel repelled by the Anthroposophical Society such as it is. Again and again one hears this opinion: 'Anthroposophy is right enough, but the anthroposophists are simply unbearable people.' We come face to face with the practical consequences almost every day.

It would be very difficult to do, through the Society, those things which must be done for the cultivation of Anthroposophy, if the Society did not reveal an understanding for the greatest possible broad-mindedness, combined, however, with the greatest zeal. *The anthroposophical cause will not abide intolerance, or narrow-mindedness—or slackness.*

You see it today on every hand: those human societies which have a spiritual substance are vigorously cultivating the human bond they have attained by virtue of their spiritual substance. Great world-embracing groups of human beings begin once more to work, and in the keenest way, because this time is the time of great decisions in the hearts of men.

The Anthroposophical Society can become a real factor in our time, if only the aforesaid intentions are received and understood by its members.

Now above all, it must become more clear how the relation of the individual member to the Anthroposophical Society should be conceived. I have said it countless times: What we may call the teaching and the spiritual impulses of this Society can be understood by every one if only he will use his everyday human intelligence. To understand what comes before the world as Anthroposophy, you do not need, for instance, any kind of Initiation or the like. All that comes out before the world can be understood, if only you are adequately open-minded. This open-mindedness, no doubt, is not an easy matter in our time, because humanity has almost lost connection with the spiritual world. Wherever you may look today, you meet with judgments such as I will now describe. Somebody says: 'There is a spiritual world, no doubt, but the spiritual world is the great mystery. Human intelligence is not fitted to gain insight into it.' Nay, it is even considered characteristic of a true way of looking to the spiritual world, to represent it as a great mystery. That which you cannot know—which you can but dimly divine, which you can only feel, and so forth—that is regarded as the truly spiritual. People do not like to admit that the spiritual can be clearly seen and understood. Most people have not the necessary courage. They find it comforting to say: The spiritual world is that which a man divines but cannot understand—it is the great secret.

Now Spiritual Science always consists in the unveiling of this secret—so that the secret is made manifest before the world. Moreover we may truly say: the one large institution (though its own members do not always recognise the fact) which is in reality inclined to place the secret before the world and make it manifest, is the Catholic Church.

Rightly understood, the Catholic Church is not in the least inclined to say that the content of the spiritual world should not be expressed in concepts and ideas. The very essence of the Catholic Church depends on the expressing in concepts of that which is a secret—which, to begin with, is hidden— for the sense-world. Indeed it is only in the last few centuries that the attitude I just described has become prevalent: and in our time it must disappear. We must recognise once more that it is precisely the task of humanity to attain the unveiling of that which is mysterious and secret.

In the 1880s, when I encountered many of the then members of the so-called 'Theosophical Society', among them were members belonging to the most intimate circles of that Society. There one could hear, again and again, the words 'abysmally profound'. Sometimes the simplest propositions were adduced with the remark that they could not, after all, be understood by men, for they were 'abysmally profound'. And if you asked one of these people, how *he* conceived the matter, he would reply: 'I cannot say—it is abysmally profound.' The Anthroposophical Society can never do with this way of talking round the secret and only emphasising that it is mysterious. The Anthroposophical Society should see that every single member may really make himself acquainted with that which Anthroposophy can give about the spiritual world. There could be no other object in his becoming a member. To begin with, he should try to gain an understanding of what can here be given. That, surely, is not much to ask. (There must, of course, be no pedantry. The guiding lines which I now give are not to be pedantically followed. Exceptions there must always be. Many exceptions will be necessary in one sense or another.) But, for two years, one should endeavour to find one's bearings in all that the Anthroposophical Society already contains, in as much as its teachings and impulses have now been developed for years past. Whoever has not been in the Society for two years, will not be well advised to enter a Class at once. It will be better for him if he does not think about that at all, but gives his mind to cultivating what is already there as Anthroposophy—there is indeed enough of it.

In saying this, I come now to the very essence of the Anthroposophical Society, which I indicated briefly in the third section of my address to members, in the *Weekly News.** Looked at externally, you may say: 'What Anthroposophy has to give is contained in books and public lectures. I can learn to know all that, for myself.' So indeed every one can, and no objection can fundamentally be made if any one takes this attitude. It will do no harm. On the contrary, it will be good if there are very many people in the world who remain at this standpoint, saying: 'I need no Society—I shall concern myself with what is given in the literature, or whatever else of Anthroposophy finds its way to the public.'

But the Anthroposophical *Society* exists to make Anthroposophy alive. This is what justifies the existence of the Society as such, in spite of the fact that Anthroposophy is already there. Anthroposophy must *live* among men. At this point we should consider what it really means, to pursue a spiritual aim

* See Vol. I, *Letters to the Members,* pp. 18-21.

in common with other human beings—for it means a very great deal indeed.

One goes into a group of the Anthroposophical Society. There, in a more or less skilful or unskilful way, something is being brought forward which the one who enters has long been familiar with; which he has read, here or there. Now there is something wrong with the Society if such a member goes away with the judgment: 'I need not have gone at all, for I already knew what they were saying.' In the realm of the Anthroposophical Society, it must be possible for true feelings to make themselves felt, as judgments. In eating, people do not generally say: 'I need not eat any chicken today, for I already know what chicken tastes like. I know the effect of chicken on my palate—why should I eat it? I am already quite familiar with its effect upon me.' That would be non-sense, would it not? But it should likewise be impossible for the judgment to arise:'Why need I go to the anthroposophical members' meetings, for I already know what is given there?'

If the true feeling is to arise in this respect, then you must go into the Society, or into its several groups, not merely in order to learn what is there said or even debated, but *simply because the human beings are there. You must be able to go there for the sake of human beings.*

This must be thoroughly understood. You go to the Anthroposophical Society not merely to be instructed, but to be together with the human beings who are there—in the Society or in its groups. Whether or not the Society prospers, depends on our feelings for the life of Anthroposophy in human souls—not merely in our own but in human souls generally. Otherwise it will always remain so: the people who are in the Society will go to its meetings in the hope of learn-ing something; and when they want to find human beings they will go to 5 o'clock teas, or other things which shall be nameless—where they come nearer to one another. The human being needs the human being. In the Anthroposophical

Society it must not be, that one does not go there for the human beings' sake. We should see to it, that we go to the meetings for the sake of the human beings in whom Anthroposophy is living. Quite a new element will thereby come into the life of Anthroposophy in the Society—an element it cannot do without, namely the purely *human*. These things are being called for most intensely at the present time.

During our Christmas Meeting, you will remember, we asked that certain persons should write and tell us their experiences of the spiritual life in the world at large. We asked them to write to Herr Steffen as editor of the *Weekly News* and of the *Goetheanum Weekly* telling of their experiences of the spiritual life, both within and without the Society.

The suggestion has already to some extent been followed, and very interesting things have come in,—albeit things that were not unknown to us. The following is an example. There is the religious community for the renewal of the Christian life, which, as you know, received its impulses out of the Anthroposophical Movement. Though it works as a separate body, it was from the Anthroposophical Movement that it received its impulses. Quite recently, this Community arranged a conference in Cassel. The gathering to begin with showed this peculiar feature, quite characteristic of our time. Those who attended it were very young, or well advanced in years. Most of the people, our reporter says, were either in or under the early twenties, or else they were older—from 35-38 years upwards. The middle age in human life—those in the twenties and early thirties—was practically absent. This, as I said, is characteristic. You will have observed it on all hands if your eyes were open. In all important matters, in all important decisions in the world in recent years, precisely those on whom the thing especially depends—namely the people between 20-22 and 38—were lacking. I do not say that the others do not matter, but it is most important to have the people of this age, for precisely their presence would enable others—namely those younger and older than they—to do something effective also. If you omit those who are in this important period of life—the importance of which you can gather from many an anthroposophical indication—things are exceedingly difficult.

None the less, many interesting things emerged at this Cassel meeting. The meeting, as I said, was entirely arranged by the Christian Community, the *Christengemeinschaft*. To begin with, the people there were shown the way, circle by circle, to the higher truths, to all that the Christian Community has to say from an independent religious standpoint. Then followed what the Christian Community also contains, namely the religious ritual. Practically the whole week had been spent in this way—I think it was from Wednesday until Sunday, when the ritual was celebrated. After this, there were two or three more days for free, informal discussion. It emerged that through all these days those present had risen—out of the real and intense need of the human heart in our time—to the holy ritual. And at the end they all asked the same question: 'Surely there must be something more, to which one must be able to come. All this can only have been a preparation, there must be something more to which one must be able to come.' So it emerged that what they were asking for was Anthroposophy. Indeed in all probability many beautiful results will emerge from this Youth Meeting in Cassel. For example, just as the Christian Community has conceived a renewal of religious life, so now an educational renewal may be conceived. Something important might arise, if with all the forces we already have, we set to work on an *Educational* renewal.

I gave this instance because you can see from it that Anthroposophy proceeds not from anyone's arbitrary desire but from that for which the human soul today is longing. If you prepare the souls to begin with through the way of feeling, they will inevitably come to the point where they no longer let the secret remain vague and nebulous but really desire to take hold of the secret unveiled, as it is in Anthroposophy.

The Anthroposophical Society must no longer be such as to hinder this carrying-out into the world of what the world is calling for—what countless hearts and souls are asking for. Therefore, in the Christmas Foundation Meeting, it has been conceived as a fully public Society.

All that can be given to begin with can be clearly recognised and understood—partly by way of understanding, partly by way of feeling. It need only be there, it need only come forward, and our Anthroposophy as well as its educational element can be seen and understood by every unprejudiced man. He need but apply his healthy human intelligence. He only must not let it be strait-jacketed by prevailing prejudices. Thus the Anthroposophical Society must be founded on insight and *on nothing else than insight*. You cannot expect anyone who is merely in the Anthroposophical Society, to make himself a bearer of Anthroposophy or a positive worker. The individual member is fully justified in simply taking the attitude that he is looking in the first place for Anthroposophy, and secondly for anthroposophical *people* in the Society. Of a member of the Anthroposophical Society, you have no immediate claim that he should do anything for the spread of Anthroposophy.

Moreover, what I wrote in one of my Letters to Members* in the *Weekly News* must also become absolutely true. You cannot spread the Anthroposophical Movement by agitation in the ordinary sense of the word. All agitation is harmful. In the domain of Anthroposophy you have no need to agitate. You only need give the people what they are already asking for. Only you must find the ways whereby they will express their longings to you. They will express them least of all if you come forward with the air of a highly learned person who declares: 'This, which has become my conviction, you too must believe, otherwise you are a fool. Everyone who does not believe what I believe is stupid.'

* See Vol. I, *Letters to Members,* p. 17.

We have not the right to give people anything else than
what they themselves are longing for. It is most important
for us to gain this spirit. We have no right to place ourselves
above the people to whom we have something to bring. We
must wean ourselves of the habit of appearing in a doctrinal
fashion or as agitators. We must be able to make it true, that
insight—pure insight—is the fundamental element of the life
of the Anthroposophical Society.

But the Anthroposophical Society must also be adminis-
tered—that is to say, the spiritual treasure must be adminis-
tered, and to this end human beings are needed. This too has
had to be provided for by the Christmas Foundation Meeting.
And those who support and sustain the administration of the
spiritual treasure must be precisely those who come into the
Classes, who will attach themselves in so doing to the Executive or *Vorstand* that has been chosen, and to the leaders at
the Goetheanum. You see, my dear friends, to *understand*
Anthroposophy, confidence or trust is not needed, but for
the administration of Anthroposophy, it should go without
saying, you must have the fullest confidence and trust in the
human beings who have this work to do. Precisely where the
classification into Classes begins, there must be the atmosphere
of complete confidence. It is on confidence that we must build.
There is no contradiction in this. Have I not said it again and
again, ever since the Anthroposophical Society has existed:
'Anthroposophy itself is to be accepted, not on the basis of
authority or trust, but on the basis of true insight. At the
same time, the administration of the anthroposophical cause
can only be founded on trust and confidence.'

There must be full human confidence in those who have
any work to undertake or to do, or any particular branch of
the work to cultivate. Thus, while on the one hand we must
conceive in the largest and most broad-minded spirit the
Anthroposophical Society itself, within the Class this question
of trust and confidence must be taken most earnestly. If only

for this reason, it is incumbent on everyone who wishes to belong to the Class to ask himself whether he really wishes to become one of those who from the outset will not only stand for the anthroposophical cause before the world but will represent it with all courage and in every way.

That esoteric deepening, of which you may read so much in my book *Knowledge of the Higher Worlds and its Attainment,* and of which so much is spoken, will have to be brought about henceforth by way of the three Classes. But this cannot be, unless the members of the Classes feel themselves as representatives of the anthroposophical cause, unless they earnestly ask themselves if they are prepared to take it on themselves to represent the anthroposophical cause before the world, in one way or another. Not everyone, needless to say, can represent it in its totality. That is neither necessary nor even expedient. I mean, to represent it in one sphere or another. Whoever would do so must, however, take his stand on the ground of complete trust and confidence. I do not say confidence in Anthroposophy itself; I mean that confidence which is indispensable for the administration of the Anthroposophical Movement.

I come to another thing, which I referred to in the third chapter of my Letters to Members.* I called it 'playing at esotericism'. This 'playing at esotericism' resulted, to a large extent, from earlier conditions in the Anthroposophical Society, and it must absolutely cease. You may take it to apply in the very widest sense. The esoteric life is a deeply serious matter, both in relation to the soul, to the human being as individual, and to the Time as a whole. Not that the necessary earnestness is achieved by 'pulling a long face' or being sentimental and self-important. There must be that inner earnestness which is by no means inconsistent with a goodly humour. To take an instance, there must be an end to the mannerism: 'I know this or that truth but I cannot tell it

* *op. cit.* p. 20.

to you, you are not yet ripe to receive it.' Apart from the fact
that you call forth the strangest feelings by such airs, you make
yourself absurdly self-important and you are not aware that
you are making yourself important.

Doubtless there are things that need to be cultivated in
narrow circles, but they cannot be treated in this way. Moreover, esoteric matters are not there to be chatted about as has
so frequently been done, or to be spread about by idle talking. These things are not at all easy to describe, for they arise
out of a fundamental attitude in life. My meaning will be
understood quickly enough in certain quarters. Esoteric
teachings are not given merely to enable us to talk, saying
that this or that was a secret of the old Mysteries, or that
there was this or that incarnation. They must be treated with
the greatest imaginable earnestness, and with a certain insight
into the following. How frequently we hear this way of talking: 'Ah! those people, they are pursuing this or that activity.
You can do nothing really esoteric with them. Let us pursue
the esoteric life among ourselves, among us worthy people.'
This attitude in itself does endless harm—to the destruction
of the Anthroposophical Society. In the first place, it is generally no more than the satisfaction of an unavowed desire for
cliques. In the second place, they who speak so have no idea
of the rich esoteric content which life itself has to offer in
every one of its branches. For life itself is esoteric through and
through. You would not believe how much esoteric life there
is in a University laboratory for example. The professors
and their assistants are unaware of it, but it is there none the
less. Esoteric life does not consist in our looking down on
this or that, and cultivating what happens to please our fancy.
It consists in our ability to get thoroughly to grips with life
and with the depths of life.

This is what I mean by 'playing at esotericism'. After all,
these things evaporate very quickly. Out of a hidden craving
for cliques you found this or that circle; it quickly evaporates.

You find it too difficult to get to grips with the esoteric content of life itself; you find it comfortable to talk about the esoteric. When esotericism passes from mouth to mouth, no matter with what unction, then it is idle esoteric chatter. I say again, this among other things does untold harm. It tends to the destruction of the Anthroposophical Society, nay of the anthroposophical cause itself.

Therefore within the Classes, in future, the question of trust and confidence will have to be taken most earnestly. It will be quite invalid for people to say: 'Having been in the Society for two years I now have a claim to be received into a Class.' For if you are received into one of the Classes, it means that the leaders of the Anthroposophical Society are obliged to work with you. The leaders cannot be enslaved, they cannot be compelled to work with those with whom they do not want to work, because—to put it plainly—they cannot work with them. Therefore—and this too it is now my duty to point out—the Christmas Foundation Meeting must also be taken in full earnestness in this respect. To those who do not find their way to be true representatives of the anthroposophical cause, it must be possible for the leaders of the School of Spiritual Science to say: 'In the General Anthroposophical Society you are most welcome, that goes without saying, but a member of the Class, unhappily, you cannot be.' There must be this possibility for the future, and I say again, it must be taken most earnestly.

Needless to say, these things will never be done out of sympathies or antipathies of any kind. They will not be done with frivolity but in true earnestness. But they must also be met with understanding. When members of the School act against the leaders, what I have just indicated will have to take effect. Every one has his several desires, naturally. One man desires this, another that. No member of the General Anthroposophical Society can be prevented from having his or her particular desires. Otherwise you will make the

Anthroposophical Society what it must not and cannot be, namely a sect or a secret society. That it must never be.

Nor will the Classes themselves bear the stamp of a secret society. Secret societies are impossible nowadays; our time calls for quite different things. But it must be possible for the leaders to work only with those with whom they *can* work. Therefore, in future, of those who desire to belong to a Class it will have to be required that in all anthroposophical matters they will communicate with the Vorstand, whenever they do anything out of their own initiative in anthroposophical matters. For only in this way will the Vorstand be able to feel itself responsible for the whole Anthroposophical Society. The Vorstand wants to feel itself responsible, it wants to stand for the whole Anthroposophical Movement.

In future it will not do for anyone to come and say: 'What we are doing is no concern of the Vorstand.' Needless to say they can do as they please, but in that case they cannot belong to the Classes. This principle of unity and consistency is a necessity. Such a spirit is just as essential in our School as it was in all the Mysteries in all the ages. Otherwise our anthroposophical life would always remain incomplete, unable to attain its goal. These are the natural laws and requirements.

Of course, any one may say: 'I wish to destroy the anthroposophical cause.' Well and good, he is free to do so, but you cannot expect those who desire to conduct the cause of Anthroposophy to admit that the first essentials of its very existence should remain unfulfilled.

Therefore, be it the arrangement of a Group or whatsoever else, such things will have to be done by the members of the Classes of the School of Spiritual Science in harmony and agreement with the leaders at the Goetheanum, so that the latter will in fact be centralising the guidance and leadership of the anthroposophical cause.

Whoever wishes to gain entry merely for the sake of curiosity, or in the hope of hearing something different in the

Classes than he can hear in the General Society, should therefore think again and rather decide not to seek entry. It was no mere figure of speech when it was said at the Christmas Meeting: 'A new impulse must now enter the life of the Society.' Of course, it will be no question of adopting mysterious airs with the profound knowledge of the Class. The point is that those who are in the Class should become the true representatives of the anthroposophical cause, and the higher the Class they are in, the more will it have to be so. The anthroposophical cause must be real and substantial. It cannot sail in the clouds, it must be absolutely real. Therefore it will not do for all manner of things to be set in motion behind the backs of the Vorstand. The care of the anthroposophical cause will be in the hands of the School of Spiritual Science. The School will not be a secret society; it will take good care that people always know, in the very widest sense, what it is doing. But the membership of it, as of the Anthroposophical Society itself, can only be based on a real foundation. For the Society, the foundation of membership is that you wish to cultivate Anthroposophy in society with other men and women. But the School of Spiritual Science will impose on its members increasingly stern obligations, otherwise it would have no substance—it would be meaningless. For example, it will be one of these obligations to discontinue what has already taken place to an unbelievable extent. I mean, to discontinue criticising in every conceivable direction those who by virtue of their qualities, have responsible posts to fill in our Anthroposophical Society. It is far too easy to criticise; to create is infinitely more difficult. When you are comfortably pursuing your daily life, providing only for your own immediate and personal concerns, you can easily criticise those who have to spend their days in doing things which must, after all, be done in the Anthroposophical Society. In this direction too, we must have another spirit Think, above all, of what is really being done in the Society. Divert the question from the issue of what is *not* to your liking. Most of the talk nowadays is of the things that are not to one's liking. Surely the main thing is to be conscious of the things that are really getting done. This should become the prevailing consciousness of our members. We do not by any means intend to claim a false principle of authority on behalf of the leaders, but in a certain respect it is but right and true: the leaders cannot do justice to their tasks if any one and every one, quite unconcerned to see how things are actually being done, lays down the law and criticises them in all directions.

These are the things to which I wished to draw attention in this lecture. For I saw that some of our friends believed, from what they had gathered hitherto, that they need only send in their names to attend the Friday lectures too, as well as the Saturday and Sunday. That would be very convenient, no doubt. But the School of Spiritual Science must consist of those who feel themselves through and through as representatives of the anthroposophical cause. Therefore I would ask our friends to consider well when they resolve to enter the Class which will now be established to begin with. It is in this sense that we shall now try to constitute the First Class, following on the Friday, Saturday and Sunday lectures. The Second Class, from the nature of the case, can only be established after a certain lapse of time.

These were the things I wished to communicate today. I arranged for this hour because the perusal of the volume I had collected of the letters that came in up to a certain time showed me that it was not unnecessary to say what I have now ventured to say. (The letters have indeed grown into one pretty bulky volume, and they promise to grow into several more.)

I also wish to know, from every one who desires to be received into the School of Spiritual Science, how long he or she has been in the Society; for it is necessary to know this. Likewise I wish to know whether the applicant is prepared to commit himself, with respect to what I have now explained on the question of trust and confidence. I wish to know whether he is really prepared to take on obligations as a member of the Class. This much should be contained in the applications. Moreover we may have to ask those friends who are hoping for admission about any other matters which we may wish to know, in addition to what is in their letters. If, however, someone writes that he would like to hear the Friday lectures, the question itself is a little difficult, . . . for the point is not that he wishes to hear the Friday lectures; they might just as well be provided for on Sundays. The point is, whether or not he wishes to be a member of the School of Spiritual Science.

These are the things that concern the members. The division into Sections will be the affair of the leaders at the Goetheanum and will be worked out by them. We shall see to it that the branches which have to be represented will in fact be represented. But that will be in every Class. Thus, after proper agreement with the leaders, every one will be able to find satisfaction for his special needs, while in the General Section of the Anthroposophical Society he will find satisfaction for his general, spiritual needs as a human being. Those who belong to any of the other Sections will also have to belong to the all-human Anthroposophical Section, which will of course be the foundation for all the other things we do.

These things, once more, will have to be taken well into account.

III

The arrangement of the School of Spiritual Science will be as follows. Anyone wishing to take part in its work will simply notify those in charge. We shall establish the First Class to begin with; the other two will be added in due course. The members of the School need only be concerned with the division into Classes. The Sections are there to enable those in charge to meet the special efforts and desires of members in each of the three Classes. Once more therefore: one will become a member not of a Section of the School, but of a Class. None the less, he for example who seeks a deeper esoteric penetration of Medicine will be able to find it—stage by stage—through the directors of the Medical Section making the necessary arrangements. And so it will be for the other Sections, scientific and artistic.

The way in which the more specialised aims of a member of any Class will be met by the particular Section will be determined by agreement with the director of the whole School (Rudolf Steiner) and with the directors of the Section. The General Anthroposophical Section must in any case be for all members of the School, and if only for this reason, admission will have to be by Classes, not by Sections.

The School of Spiritual Science cannot be a University or College in the usual sense. It will therefore make no effort to enter into competition with these or to act as a substitute for them. But something which cannot be found in the ordinary Schools and Universities—namely, esoteric penetration—will be there for those who seek it at the Goetheanum. Here the human soul will find what it really needs in its striving for knowledge. Striving for knowledge can be a purely human thing. The General Section of the School will be for those who have the purely human need—to find the paths of the soul to the spiritual world. It will represent, for them, an Esoteric School. For those again who wish to devote themselves to special objects—scientific, artistic or otherwise—the special Sections of the School will try to open up appropriate paths. Thus every seeker shall find at the Goetheanum School what he is striving for out of the special circumstances of his life. The School is not intended as a purely scientific nor learned, but as a purely human institution. Nevertheless it must also be able to meet and fulfil the esoteric needs of the scientist, scholar and artist.

CONDITIONS FOR ADMISSION TO THE
FIRST CLASS OF THE SCHOOL OF
SPIRITUAL SCIENCE

*After the lecture given on 3 February 1924 (see Anthroposophy: an
Introduction), Dr. Steiner spoke as follows to those who had applied
for admission to the First Class:*

By being present at this meeting one does not, of course,
commit oneself to anything as yet. It will still be necessary for
each of you who has remained behind to think the matter over
thoroughly, and find out for himself if he really wants to take
on the duties that would be his if he were to become a member of the School of Spiritual Science. For you see, my dear
friends, what has often been referred to as the second condition of belonging to such an association of human beings,
must from now on be taken in all earnestness. Many in our
circles have hardly begun to understand what taking things
in earnest really implies.

We have to begin with the General Anthroposophical
Society which provides modern man with spiritual knowledge. Anyone can become a member of this, without wishing
to take on further responsibilities. There is therefore no need
to go beyond mere membership of the Society and take on
real and earnest responsibilities, unless one has the desire to
do so. But we simply must have a group of people who penetrate through the exoteric to the esoteric, and this cannot be
achieved unless one shoulders definite responsibilities. For if
none could be found to take on these responsibilities, then,
my dear friends, Anthroposophy would not be able to exist.

The basis of what I want to establish as the First Class is
that the relationship between the leaders of the School and
the individual members must be seen as a kind of mutual

contract, a contract freely entered upon, but also strictly imple-
mented. The leaders cannot at any point feel themselves
bound to work in the sense of the First Class with any member
who does not accept his obligations. So it is really a matter of
a mutual agreement freely made. But the fact of this free
mutual agreement must also be grasped as something of real
import. It is only in this way that we shall gradually become
able to enter into what is truly esoteric.

First and foremost it will be essential that all members of
the Class also state their complete willingness to cultivate
Anthroposophy in the world and to stand as its representatives. After all, the difference between what has come about
since Christmas and what existed previously is the fact that,
fundamentally speaking, the Anthroposophical Society was
previously a kind of administrative society. It received Anthroposophy as its content and was concerned with providing a
framework for it in the world.

What must now come about is that that institution which
has its centre here in Dornach and is presented to the world,
is looked upon as esoteric in character. As a consequence of
this the Executive formed at Christmas should be regarded
by members of the First Class as a body carrying full responsibility for Anthroposophy in the world. That is to say,
everything of an anthroposophical nature is the concern of
this Executive.

If you accept this in all its implications, then you will also
appreciate that it will be out of the question for things to
happen as regards true anthroposophical life such as have
already occurred here and there since Christmas. For instance,
people have been heard to say, 'Oh, we are going to do this
on our own; we are not going to the Executive about it.
Why should we trouble ourselves about the Executive?'—
Yes, indeed, my dear friends, a member of the First Class will
in future have to face the fact that if he wants to engage
in some anthroposophical activity independently of the

Executive, then the Executive will also wish to act independently of him.

I would not of course say this within the framework of the General Anthroposophical Society. But that is exactly what characterises the free mutual agreement that must exist between members of the First Class and the Executive. If there is anyone who wants to present something to the world on the basis of Anthroposophy without first getting into touch with the Executive, the Executive will have to say to him that they too on their part will want to arrange their affairs without reference to him. Admittedly, this is a special kind of relationship. It could be described in words other than those which I have just used. But only in this way can we integrate the life within the School of Spiritual Science.

In this way we shall gradually create the earnest attitude towards Anthroposophy that is needed. Then we shall be able to have a core of people who really share in the responsibility for what should come about out of Anthroposophy. Through this too it will become impossible to have among us any more cliques. For it is this desire to form cliques, the arising of cliques, that has done us untold damage. We shall also not be able to have any more one-sided and self-centred personal activities. If such things must come to expression, then they may do so within the Anthroposophical Society, but they will be impossible among those who belong to the Classes. For if Class members were to act in such a way, they would in fact cease to be members of the Class.

These are matters which we must ponder over in all seriousness. If we can take them with at least as much earnestness as many more mundane matters are taken in the world at large, then a certain reality will grow up among us. If this were not to happen, then the whole new foundation of the Society, as it has been established at Christmas, would be meaningless. You see, it has become the custom, also in the part of the Society immediately around Dornach, for members to say many a time: 'Well, we don't want to burden him. We don't want to ask his advice about every detail.'—The fact is, they have generally not asked me about those things where it suited them not to ask!

This has led to the situation that a number of undertakings have come to my notice when they had already gone a certain way. They had come to a stage where they had to be solved in a different way from that in which they would have been, had I been approached about them at the beginning. What I wish to state very clearly is that as far as the content of Anthroposophy is concerned, there must be a unified approach. Certainly difficulties will arise, for the small number of Executive members who are here will be over-burdened. All the same we shall allow things to work themselves out, we shall deal with them just as they arise. But do not let us again make the mistake of consulting the Executive in relatively unimportant matters but saying in the case of most important issues: 'We must manage on our own'—(because that is more pleasant)— 'we must not trouble the Executive!' Of course, it can be said, if one sticks to formalities, 'Yes, but where, then, is freedom?' Certainly, everyone can have his freedom, in as much as he need take no part in these things. But the Executive too must have their freedom. They too must be free to choose not to do something for which they cannot take the responsibility.

If there is sufficient good-will, the necessity of such things will be obvious. What I am saying here will give rise to a clear and definite self-examination on the part of those present as to whether they want to accept this particular obligation to have, from the beginning, this relationship of mutual trust with the Executive over everything concerning Anthroposophy. Otherwise the Executive on their part will have to make clear that they do not consider some particular matter as being anthroposophical in character. With this they also, of course, make it clear that they will not work with those who found in some place or other a special Anthroposophy of their own. This situation is really extremely important and must be taken in all seriousness.

What a great deal of talk there has been about bringing our Society into the open, especially about the fact that the lecture-courses are to be made public! My dear friends, this is a fact that cannot be taken earnestly enough! Proof of the necessity for such a measure meets one on every hand. This very morning Dr. Unger handed me a new publication by Hans Leisegang, entitled *The Occult Sciences*. It appears in the collection, Perthes Educational Library (*Perthes Bildungsbücherei*), published by one of the best-known publishers in existence—Friedrich Andreae, Berlin, Gotha, Stuttgart. All the more, therefore you can understand the importance of Leisegang's denunciation. It is printed today by one of the most reputable publishers. So it is essential to grasp these things in their full significance. There is a little slip of paper in each copy of the book, on which there appear, under the name of Mr. Leisegang, the following words: 'A spiritual revolt against the hitherto unknown lecture-courses of Rudolf Steiner. Hans Leisegang.' The book *The Occult Sciences* is an important new addition to Perthes Educational Library and provides a survey of the development and the present state of research into the field of occultism, together with an extensive bibliography for further reading. The author makes a sharp dividing-line between scientists and occultists.*

My dear friends, even had it not already been done, it is quite obvious that the lecture-courses would straightaway have to be declared public in face of such a statement. 'A spiritual revolt against the hitherto unknown lecture-courses of Rudolf Steiner!' Well, it has been done already. For in a very thorough, fundamental, and even violent way, our opponents make even the most recent lecture-courses their con-

---

* At this point a sentence is unfortunately missing from the shorthand report.

cern. No sooner has a lecture-course appeared than they have it already in their hands, and discuss it. To be sure, there is much more talk about the lecture-courses among our opponents than there is among the anthroposophists themselves. In such a situation it would obviously be paradoxical to keep the lecture-courses at all secret; this would merely mean that we deliver ourselves into the hands of our enemies.

Since the Christmas Foundation Meeting there has been a good deal of talk about making the lecture-courses available to the public. But what is entirely lacking in face of the fact that this step had to be taken, is the earnestness that such a situation demands. And I would like to say in this connection that the members of the First Class must constitute a society of anthroposophists filled with a sense of earnest responsibility.

A great deal of what has been brought about by the Christmas Meeting has not yet come to clear consciousness. It remains to be seen whether this First Class can be established in actual fact. That is why I will ask you once more—so that there can be a clear picture as regards all the friends who wish to take part in the School here at Dornach—to write your names once more, but only once, on these sheets which I will distribute here, and then to bring them back to me to this table. I will distribute these sheets, one for every two rows of chairs, and I would ask you to write your names down. Write no more than just your names, please. What I need apart from that will be contained, no doubt, in the letters you wrote. Those who did not state the length of their membership in their letters are asked to do so now in these lists.

Next Friday, then, I shall have to announce the way in which those who have been admitted are to receive their membership cards. I will now consider all these applications and we will then hand over the membership cards in a way that will, I hope, be a little more convenient for the persons concerned than was the way in which the letters of application have been handed in. They were pressed into my hand wherever people happened to meet me, right hand or left, just as opportunity offered, without considering that for some-one who has a lot of things to see to, this makes it exceedingly difficult to keep things together. One person took his letter here, the other somewhere else . . . but we hope, as I say, that we shall be able to handle the whole thing in a somewhat more orderly fashion.

IV

The member who joins this School is in a very different position from one who first enters the Anthroposophical Society. For he does not enter the School till he has been a member of the Society for a sufficiently long time. He has learned to know Anthroposophy—what it intends and what it really is. He has had ample opportunity to discover what its value for himself can be. Now this implies that the will to join can very properly be associated with the assumption of responsibilities and obligations and the conscious desire to be a representative of anthroposophical activity and influence.

Considering how Anthroposophy is presented in the Anthroposophical Society, it is not only absurd but fatuous when opponents again and again repeat the falsehood, 'Anthroposophy seeks to influence people by suggestion'. Every one who is in Anthroposophy knows the truth perfectly well, or at any rate can know it. And if some members who have left the Society still repeat the above statement, they themselves are in most cases well aware that what they are saying is objectively untrue. In the Society no one is led blindfold to Anthroposophy. No one therefore can become a member of the School who does not already stand—and with full insight —in the sphere of those purposes which Anthroposophy takes as its own.

Everyone should judge for himself—considering all that he has learned and found as a member of the Anthroposophical Society—whether he wishes to become a member of the School. If then the leaders of the School speak of duties and responsibilities devolving on its members, the latter have every opportunity to understand how this is meant. It means no more than that those in charge of the School cannot fulfil *their* tasks unless responsibilities are undertaken by its members. The relation of each member of the School to those in charge remains an absolutely free one none the less. For the leader must also enjoy the freedom to act according to the inherent conditions of his task. This freedom would be taken away from him if he were not allowed to say to each intending member—who is after all at liberty to join the School or not as he desires—'If I am to work with you, you on your side must undertake to fulfil such and such conditions.'

This should really go without saying, nor should it be necessary to explain it. But it must be stated none the less, for we hear it said only too often: 'If then one wants to join the School one must forfeit something of one's human freedom!' When members of the Society can speak like this it is hardly surprising if ill-disposed opponents utter the calumny that Anthroposophy slowly deprives its followers of their free will and makes them instruments for the shady purposes of a few individuals. But who can fail to know—having been in the Society and taken part in its work for a long enough time— that Anthroposophy would become absolutely meaningless the moment it took a single step in any direction whatsoever against the independent, the fully considered and enlightened, will of its members! With instruments deprived of their free will, Anthroposophy most assuredly can not attain its purpose. For to achieve Anthroposophy in any real sense, the free will of those who take part in it is the very first thing needed.

17 February 1924

V

The members of the School, if they accept the conditions above mentioned, will make the Anthroposophical Society a reality, which alone can justify its existence. The working centre of the School will of course have to be the Goetheanum. Here the definite work which the School has to do will first be undertaken. But ways and means will be found for members of the School scattered over the world to take a full share in its work. This will not be achieved through a furore to obtain by every conceivable means copies or notes of what is being said at the Goetheanum. Such a furore we already experienced about a year ago, when the word went forth that new life must come into the Society.

By impetuous procedure of this sort we can make no progress. On 15 February I shall hold my first lecture at the Goetheanum for the School of Spiritual Science. Those members will then be present whom the Executive has so far been able to notify of their admission to the School. Anyone who has applied for admission and has not yet been notified need not therefore regard himself as unaccepted. The whole arrangement of the School, including the matter of membership, can only emerge in course of time.

We at the Goetheanum shall have to take the necessary steps to facilitate the further spread of the work of the School; the way we shall do this will become increasingly evident as the work proceeds. Ways and means will be sought for at this place, where the School has its centre, and we shall then communicate with those persons and groups who have intimated that they desire membership. But it must be borne in mind that we at the Goetheanum shall not succeed in our objects if already existing institutions simply announce: 'We are here, and we now wish to join the Goetheanum and its School.' The declaration as such is of course good, and all that happens in this direction will be gladly welcomed by the Executive. But it does not do to say: 'We come to you as we are at this present moment; transform us here and now into members of the School.' The result of this might be that everyone would continue to do as he had done before, only re-christening his activities under the name of the School of Spiritual Science

What the Executive at the Goetheanum is working for can but gradually flow into the single institutions. The Executive does not regard 'organisation' as its task, but actual work. Its duty will then be to offer the results of its work, in a proper form, to those who want them. One may 'organise' ever so well, but in a Society like the Anthroposophical nothing is accomplished by it. The life of this Society consists in the real work that is done in it. In the participation of all members in the work at the Goetheanum lies the best guarantee for the prosperity of the Society. The Executive on the other hand will endeavour to incorporate in the Society everything that the members may accomplish.

24 February 1924

VI

To the Sections already mentioned, which the Executive of the Anthroposophical Society is seeking to establish at the Goetheanum, one more ought to be added, and this will be possible if our purpose is met with sympathy and understanding by those whom it concerns.

In every age Youth stood in a certain contrast to Old Age. Many people nowadays, observing with anxiety the symptoms of life in modern Youth, appear to find comfort in this truism. Such easy comfort may very well grow harmful.

It is out of the spirit of the time that we must understand the Youth of the time, not only in its aberrations but in its strivings—which are, alas, only too well justified—to find something different from what the older generation is giving it today.

To begin with there is that section of Youth which is brought by circumstances into academic life. Science and learning are presented to it: Science solid and secure, well knit together, applicable to external life. It would be foolish nonsense to raise an outcry—as non-scientific people often do—against this Science. And yet, Youth freezes in soul by contact with it, even if it comes to the point of appreciating the security and firmness, the fruitfulness of scientific learning.

Science owes its greatness to an intense opposition in which it took the lead since the middle of last century. At that time it was realised that we may come into complete uncertainty of knowledge if we try to climb from the lowlands of Research on to the heights of Philosophy, seeking for a comprehensive outlook on the world. Men felt that they had witnessed pretty unattractive instances of the result of such attempts.

So they set out to liberate 'true Science' from 'philosophic speculation'. Science was to keep to the facts, remaining in the lowlands of Nature and avoiding the perilous ascent to higher spiritual regions.

When the opposition was in full swing there was a certain satisfaction in it. The champions of 'Science against Speculation' in the middle of the nineteenth century were happy in their fighting mood.

The Youth of today can no longer share this happiness. Witnessing the fight against the 'uncertainty' or 'unfounded fanaticism' of loftier conceptions of the world, they can no longer stir their souls to joyful feeling. For there is nothing left to fight against! No one today can raise the battle-cry that Science must be freed from the more ambitious flights of Philosophy. For in the meantime these have died out of their own accord.

But the sensitive feeling of Youth has made a fresh discovery—not a discovery of the intellect, but one that comes from the whole and undivided nature of man. Youth today has discovered that man cannot live without a fuller and loftier conception of the world. Many of the older generation listened to the arguments against such 'theories' and submitted to the cogency of 'proof'. Intellectually, the Youth of today are no longer interested in the matter, while instinctively they feel the powerlessness of intellectual proof where the heart of man is speaking from an unconquerable impulse.

The Science presented to modern Youth is solid enough, but it owes its solidity to its lack of an all-embracing conception of the world. Youth calls for the very thing which scientific learning lacks. Yet Science needs the Youth.

We at the Goetheanum would fain understand the Youth, and prove it by seeking *together* with them the paths to a fuller conception of life and the world. And we hope that in the light of this conception the true love of scientific learning will be kindled. We do not want to lose hold on Science while we dream of loftier world-conceptions. Through a wide-awake and conscious knowledge of the Spirit we want to gain a fuller Science.

The Executive of the Anthroposophical Society asks the Youth if they on their side are prepared to meet it with understanding. If they will do so, the 'Section for the Spiritual Aspirations of Youth' will become a thing of life and strength in the School of Spiritual Science.

2 March 1924

VII

The first piece of work in the School of Spiritual Science took place during the Christmas Meeting and in connection with it. The Section of which Dr. Ita Wegman is the leader was responsible. During the last few days of the Meeting, the practising doctors who were present as members of the Anthroposophical Society came together. They formulated questions which were especially engaging their attention, and I took these as the basis of what I had to say. The leaders of the School will try to continue the work thus introduced, as opportunities allow. As soon as we can, we shall write to those concerned and indicate our possible lines of procedure.

In connection with the Christmas Meeting and in the same Section of the School a Course was given for younger doctors and medical students. Here I spoke especially of the inner attunement of soul which is necessary in those who would devote themselves to medicine. The Course was given to meet the spiritual needs which medical students, who came to the Goetheanum, had expressed. I tried to indicate what it is that a man or woman in the medical profession must aspire to know of the World and Man. At the same time I sought to reveal the sources of a true ethic of medicine—of the true 'medical spirit'. The brevity of the Course made it possible to give suggestions and outlines only. But we may hope that this beginning too will be continued.

For the General Anthroposophical Section the meetings of the First Class of the School of Spiritual Science have begun.

In the Section for the Arts of Speech and Music, under the leadership of Frau Marie Steiner, there was an inner need just at this time to arrange a Course on Tone Eurythmy. This Course* has now been given. It was attended by Eurythmy teachers and artists living at Dornach, by those from outside who were able to come, by the members of the Executive of the Anthroposophical Society, and by a few others, specially interested in Music and Eurythmy.

The substance of these lectures will be given out in a suitable form as soon as possible. Here I will say only a few words about their general bearing and intention. Hitherto, in the art

* See *Eurythmy as visible Song* (8 lectures); also *Eurythmy as visible Speech* (15 lectures).

of Eurythmy, we have brought 'Speech Eurythmy' to a certain point of development. We are the severest critics of our own efforts; we know that the most we have been able to achieve in this sphere is but a beginning. Still, a beginning has been made, and this must be followed up and carried forward.

In 'Tone Eurythmy' or 'visible song', we had not yet advanced so far as in Speech Eurythmy or the 'visible word'. To continue along the right lines with such beginnings as we had made, it was necessary—at the present stage of Tone Eurythmy practice—to give a further development. Such was the object of this Course. We had to consider at the same time the nature of Music itself. For in Eurythmy, Music becomes visible; and to make the real essence of Music visible, the Eurythmist must feel where it is in human nature that Music has its source.

In Tone Eurythmy that which lives in Music, invisibly but audibly, becomes visible. At this point there is great danger of growing unmusical. But I hope to have proved by the lectures of the recent Course that the danger is not essential. For when Music flows into visible movement the need arises to eliminate all the unmusical elements remaining in it, and to carry over into the realm of vision only the 'pure Music' itself. One who thinks that true Music must cease when the audible is transplanted into visible movement and form, will certainly have misgivings about Tone Eurythmy altogether. But we may venture to say that such an opinion is not in its deepest essence an artistic one. The man for whom Art is a living experience will be glad of every extension of artistic sources and forms of expression. And in the last resort, Music, like every true Art, has its fountain-head in the innermost nature of Man, for which the means of expression are unlimited in their variety. That in the human being which longs to sing, longs also to find expression in forms of movement. In Speech or Tone Eurythmy powers of movement already

inherent in man's bodily nature are simply realised and brought
to expression. It is Man himself who reveals his nature in
Eurythmy. The human form can only be understood as
frozen movement—movement brought to rest. The inner
meaning of the human form lies unrevealed until the human
being moves. Thus, we may truly say, to dispute the justifica-
tion of Tone or Speech Eurythmy is to refuse to allow full
human nature to reveal itself.

Materialism does indeed refuse to allow the Spirit to reveal
itself in human knowledge. And the refusal to admit Eurythmy as an Art existing alongside of and working in co-
operation with the other Arts, springs—we may presume—
from a like attitude of mind.

We hope that the Eurythmists found fresh stimulus and
help in the Course, and that something may have been done
thereby for the further development of the Art.

9 March 1924

THE YOUTH SECTION IN THE SCHOOL OF SPIRITUAL SCIENCE

VIII

What I have to say on this Matter to the Older Members

The announcement of a 'Section for the Spiritual Aspirations
of Youth' in the Goetheanum School has met with very
gratifying response. Representatives of the 'Free Anthroposophical Society', and also the younger members living at
the Goetheanum, have expressed to the Executive of the
Anthroposophical Society their wholehearted readiness to
take part.

I see in this a valuable point of departure for what will form a very beautiful part of the work of our Society. If the Society can make a bridge between the older and the younger men and women of our time, it will have achieved a thing of great importance.

We can read between the lines, in both of these communications, something which we may sum up in these words: Youth is now speaking in a manner which strikes a new note in the evolution of mankind. We feel they are not looking so much for a continuance of what has been inherited from the past, hoping for its further evolution in the present. They are turning toward the inrush of new life from spheres where it is not *Time* which evolves things but *Eternity* which brings them forth.

If the older man today wishes to be understood by the young, he must somehow make the Eternal the driving force in his relation to things temporal. And he must do so in a way the young can understand.

It is said that the young will not look to the old—will accept nothing of the insight and ripe experience which they have gained. So says the older person, in his annoyance at the spirit of modern youth.

It is true, the young draw back from the old, they want to be among themselves. They will not give ear to what Old Age has to say.

These facts may well occasion anxiety. For the young people will in their turn be old. They will not always be able to act in this spirit. They want to be 'truly young'; their question is, how to be young in the true sense. Yet this will no longer be possible for them when they themselves have grown old.

Therefore—so thinks the older person—Youth should abandon its pretensions, and look up once more to Age, to direct its spiritual life along the right channels.

Those who speak thus evidently think it is the fault of the young that they are not attracted to the old. And yet, the young could not help looking up to their elders and taking them as their example if their elders were 'old' in a true way. For the human soul is so constituted that it turns to what is unfamiliar and different from itself, seeking union with this.

But Youth today does not see in the older men and women any human quality different from its own yet worthy of its emulation. For the older man of the present day is not really 'old'. He has taken in the content of many things and can talk of these. But his knowledge has not ripened in him. He has grown older in years, but in his soul he has not kept pace with his advancing years. He speaks out of an older brain just in the same way as he spoke when his brain was young. The Youth feel this fact. They do not perceive maturity when they are with their elders; they see their own, young state of soul in older bodies. And they turn away, for this does not seem true to them.

For many decades past the older generation has developed the idea that 'it is not possible to have knowledge' about the Spiritual in the things and events of the world. When the young hear this, the feeling is bound to arise in them that the old people have nothing to give them. After all, they can manage the 'not knowing' for themselves. They will hearken to the old when they feel that the old have real knowledge to convey.

To talk about 'not knowing' is tolerable when it is done with freshness, with youthfulness. But to listen to this talk about 'not knowing' when it proceeds from brains grown old, empties the soul—expecially the youthful soul.

If Youth turns away from the older people, it is not because they are 'old' but because they have stayed 'young'. They have failed to grow old in the true sense. This is a piece of self-knowledge very necessary for the older folk today.

It is only possible to become old in the real way if one lets the Spirit unfold within one's soul. If one does so, then the aged body will contain something that harmonises with it. Then one will have a real gift to offer Youth. *It will not be what Time's evolving course has made of the Body, but what Eternity is making manifest out of the Spirit.*

Where there is an earnest seeking for conscious experience of Spirit, there is the sphere in which Youth and Age can meet once more. It is an empty phrase to say 'We must be young with the young'. No, to be with Youth, we older people must understand how to be truly old.

The young like to criticise what comes from the older generation. In this they are perfectly right. For the time will come when they must carry human progress forward to a point the old have not yet reached. But old age is untrue if it merely joins in this criticism. The young may let it pass for a time; it saves them the annoyance of contradiction. But in the end they grow tired of these old-youthful people, finding their voice too harsh. There is more life in criticism when the voice is young.

Anthroposophy, in its search for the Spiritual in life, wishes to find a field in which the young can gladly meet the old. The Executive of the Anthroposophical Society is happy that its announcement has been so warmly welcomed by the Youth. But the active members of the Anthroposophical Society must not leave the Executive in the lurch. For simultaneously with the assent from one side, I received a communication from another, containing words which *must* be listened to by those whose heart is in this Society: 'The day', it said, 'might come when we young folk would have to free ourselves from the Anthroposophical Society, just as you once had to free yourselves inwardly from the Theosophical Society.'

Such a day would certainly come if we in the Anthroposophical Society were unable to realise in the near future what the announcement of a 'Section for the Young' implies. It is to be hoped that the active members will work with the Executive at the Goetheanum in this matter, so that the day may rather come when the young will say, 'We will unite ourselves always ever more closely with all that is Anthroposophy.'

This time I have spoken to the older members of the Anthroposophical Society about the Youth. In the next number I wish to say what it lies on my heart to say to the Youth themselves.

16 March 1924

IX

What I have to say on this Matter to the Younger Members

When I announced the founding of a Youth Section, the Committee of the 'Free Anthroposophical Society' addressed a letter to their members. In it they pointed out that I considered 'the true concerns of Youth' important enough to be the object of a special branch of spiritual-scientific training. I do indeed; and anyone who reads the description of my life in the *Goetheanum Weekly* will understand the reason. When I was as young as those who now write this letter, I was alone and lonely in the same condition of soul which, as I find, is widespread among the Youth of today. My companions in youth felt differently at the time. This civilisation, of which the letter says that none of its callings or professions are any longer a channel to lead the Youth to a fuller and loftier conception of the world, and that the innate idealism of Youth can no longer find expression in its callings—this civilisation was then in the ascendant. My companions in youth felt in it the flower of the newest stage in human progress. They felt themselves freed from the pretentious vanities of the old striving for loftier conceptions. They felt themselves strong and happy in the prospect of professions built on the 'secure foundations of science'.

I too saw the flowering of this civilisation. But I could not

63

help feeling that it would bear no truly human fruit. My companions did not feel as I did. They were carried along by the joyful experience of it. They did not yet miss the fruit, for they spent their enthusiasm in the happy vision of the unfruitful flower.

Now it is all different. The flower is faded, and instead of any fruit a strange and hostile growth is revealed, causing the humanity of man to freeze. The Youth of today feel the coldness of a civilisation which is void of a spiritual conception of the world.

A surface layer of consciousness was alive in the companions of my youth. In this surface layer they could delight in the unfruitful flower, whose unfruitfulness was as yet unrevealed. And it was a splendid flower in its way. Their delight in its effulgence eclipsed the deeper layers of their consciousness—those layers where the longing for true humanity lives unquenchable in every human being. The youth of today, now that the flower is faded, can no longer take delight in it. The surface layer of consciousness is bare and barren, and the deeper layers are exposed. The longing for a conception of the world stands revealed in their hearts today and threatens grievously to wound their inner life.

I would say to the Youth of today; 'Do not blame the old too harshly—the old who forty years ago along with me were young.' Certainly there are superficial ones among them, who even now will vainly flaunt their emptiness as a form of superiority. But there are also those among them who bear their fate with resignation, for fate indeed has denied them the living and conscious experience of their true humanity.

Fate set them here in the final phase of the Dark Age—the age which in the conscious experience of the material world was digging the grave of the living Spirit.

Youth is now placed beside the grave and the grave is empty, for the Spirit cannot die—cannot be buried.

To be young has become a riddle for those who experience

it today, for in the very fact of Youth their longing for the Spirit is laid bare. But the Light Age has dawned. If it is not yet felt, it is that most men still bear in their souls the after-effects of the old darkness. But any man who has a sense for the realities of Spirit can feel that the Light is here.

The Light will only become perceptible to men when the great riddles of existence are born again in a new way. And of these one of the first is the riddle of Youth. How are we to experience Youth in a world which has grown rigid in sene-scence? Such is the unspoken question which lives in the feel-ing of the young men and women of today.

Because Youth has thus become a human riddle, it can have a special branch of spiritual-scientific training as a living attempt to solve the riddle.

In this training we shall not spend our time in empty phrases about Youth. But we shall seek the light which must fall upon our life in youth—so that the Youth may recognise itself in its humanity.

To be young today is to call irresistibly for a fuller vision of the world, such as may fill our life-work and vocation with the warmth it needs. To be young today is to recoil from the professions which a civilisation void of a loftier conception has evolved. To be young today is to want to see our life-work—our professions—grow out of humanity, instead of being forced to witness the killing of our humanity in our professions.

If we are to find our place in the world without losing our own human being in the effort, we need a living relation-ship-of-soul to the world, and this can only be awakened in the experience of a fuller, loftier conception of the world. Such were the thoughts and feelings of the Executive of the Anthroposophical Society in making their announcement. In this spirit we should like to unite the younger anthroposo-phists in a Youth Section, wherein they may work towards a truly human and creative life.

But there is one more thing I would say to our younger members. If we succeed in giving the Youth Section its proper substance, those in the anthroposophical life who have known how to grow old in the true way will want to make common cause with the Youth. Let the Youth not say when this happens, 'We will not sit down to a common table with the old people'. For Anthroposophy should be no thing of age. It lives in the Eternal which brings all men together. Let the Youth find full scope for their youth in the Anthroposophical Society. And the old, if they take Anthroposophy into their nature in a full and living way, will feel themselves drawn to the Youth. They will find that what they gained by age can be imparted best of all to Youth. And the young themselves will vainly struggle for the true humanity if they shun that humanity which they, too, must enter in due time. As the world runs its course, the old must be made young ever and again, for otherwise it would lose all life and being. Among the true older anthroposophists the Youth will find what they require, lest they themselves one day should reach an old age of their own which they would want in vain to flee away from.

23 March 1924

X

What I yet have to say on this matter to the Younger Members

Wherever the Youth Movement makes its appearance today, its draws its life from a certain privation. What is it that the young man of today lacks, what does he feel himself deprived of, when the fact of his youth comes home to him? Surely there is so much to learn in the civilisation of today. It contains a fullness—nay, a superfluity of things worthy to be known.

One might readily imagine that the Youth of today are perplexed, distracted by this very fullness, unable to understand all that it brings to them. But experience shows that this idea is wrong. Our young men and women understand perfectly well what this civilisation places before them. One can always understand what can be grasped in thought; and our present civilisation, despite its superfluity, can—almost exhaustively—be grasped in thought.

As soon as they begin to gain a relationship to it, our young folk become aware that they understand this civilisation perfectly well. And a true instinct tells them that such understanding—grasping of things in thought—will henceforth be their destiny. But 'understanding' of this kind does not go with youthfulness. To be youthful is to experience with an overflowing heart, with all one's soul, things which one will only understand in the future. Gradually, as the things he experiences so fully become objects of understanding for him, the young man divines that he is growing old.

The Youth of today receive from civilisation something with which one can indeed grow old but with which one can not be young. This civilisation has practically nothing to give to the first age in life. One ought really to come to the earth aged twenty years today; then one could permeate oneself with what modern civilisation contains.

It has lost the Spirit. It brings only material things into its thoughts; and such thoughts cannot be livingly experienced, they can only be 'understood'. Once understood, they lie in the soul like stones—hard and incapable of change. For in their very origin they are already complete and mature, hence they cannot grow. But the young human being must grow, and he wants what he takes into his soul to grow with him.

A real Science of the Spirit—that too can only reveal itself in thoughts. But its thoughts are concrete; they can be seen, they can be experienced, and no one can receive them in a more mature condition than his own maturity. They are akin to man's own being, and thus they grow and ripen with him. If I am a boy or girl of eighteen years, and someone gives me thoughts from the material sphere of life, I receive the thoughts in much the same way as I should do if I were aged forty or fifty. But if by the very expression of his humanity he makes me experience thoughts that spring forth fresh from the Spirit, he may be seventy years old; I with my eighteen years will harmoniously unite them with my eighteen year-old condition and they will grow with me as I grow.

The materialistic conception and mode of thought really demands that Youth should fill itself with things of old age. But Youth wants to experience what it is to be young; and so, forced as it is to experience old age, Youth today suffers privation. The Youth Section at the Goetheanum would like to give the Youth a knowledge which is alive and with whose life they can livingly take hold of their own youthfulness. The civilisation of today has no thoughts with which youthfulness could be experienced, but a true Science of the Spirit will indeed have such thoughts.

An older man, hearing the young people speak, will often have the feeling nowadays, 'How old do their speeches sound!' although they come from youthful lips. These ways of speech the young men of today have found among the old. They take them up but do not unite them with their own nature. Trying to experience them, they feel untrue to themselves. They utter things which in them cannot be true, while they bear the truth of their own nature hidden within them, unable to reveal it even to themselves. It suffocates them; it becomes like a nightmare, pressing on them from within.

Freedom to breathe in the living Life of the Spirit is what the Youth are wanting, so that the incubus may pass away from them. They want to awaken in a healthy perception of the Spirit, so that their consciousness may be filled with the real experience of youth.

Youth would like to be awake in their youth. But the

thoughts of a materialistic civilisation will only let them dream of it. Now man cannot dream without darkening his consciousness. So the Youth-consciousness must wander about through the mechanical world of present-day reality in a dim and dreaming state. Its hammer-blows and its electric waves beat into the dream but cannot call it to awakening. For they are not human, they are extra-human.

But Spiritual Science is there for souls who want to be awake. Spiritual Science not only wants to give knowledge to man, but to bring him life. It will then be for his own free activity to change this life into knowledge.

People who imagine they are poets, though they are really pedants, will object, Do not deprive Youth of their dreams! Do not awaken them or you will rob them of the very best of youth. He who speaks thus does not know that dreams attain their full value only when the light of the waking consciousness illumines them. Mechanical civilisation does not call forth the dreams of youth to glad radiance and light, but grinds them down even as they arise, making of them a burden and an oppression.

It is only in pictures of this kind that we can say what the Youth Section wishes to achieve. It will publish no programme. It will issue no manifesto as to the Real Nature of Youth. It will try to let life arise from what its founders themselves can experience of the privations of the young men and women of today. The result of this will be a wisdom of youth, unfolding itself daily anew.

Young men and women living at the Goetheanum made known their will to work in the Youth Section as soon as it was announced, and they have not ceased to do so. Enthusiasm speaks in all their words. In my first statement I said that the Youth Section will be effective if its real idea is understood; and I do believe that enthusiasm can bring about true understanding—not that 'understanding' of which I have just spoken, which spells privation to the Youth, but a very different understanding (though the same word is used to denote it) namely an understanding born not of the intellect but of the full human being.

The Executive of the Anthroposophical Society can long for nothing else than to feel itself face to face with the receptiveness of true enthusiasm. For then it may hope that the living power of Spiritual Science will be sufficient to give to enthusiasm what enthusiasm longs to carry on its wings. The Executive would like to live with the Youth in such a way that they can join their youth, in a true human way, with age. For it believes that it will thus perceive and supply the very thing which the Youth are lacking and for which they long with all their hearts.

30 March 1924

ON THE YOUTH SECTION IN THE SCHOOL OF SPIRITUAL SCIENCE

XI

Once more I wish to address myself to our younger friends in the Anthroposophical Society concerning the Youth Section. In the Youth circles among us there seem to be two different opinions. One of them feels that true youthfulness must be on the quest for something. It feels drawn to Anthroposophy because here it hopes to find satisfaction in its quest. It has awakened to the fact that the quest of Youth must go to the depths of the soul, and the civilisation of today cannot lead to the depths. There is a section among the Youth, seeking in this way for an esoteric life because they have dimly discovered that here alone the true nature of man can be consciously experienced.

This section of the Youth will readily find their way to that which the Executive intends with the Youth Section of the School. And the Executive will never interfere with anyone in his independent striving. It will have a warm heart for every kind of independence. But it will also remember that the cultivation of esoteric life has come to it as its own task. This will be its first care. It will guide the Youth Section in such a way that true esoteric life may come into its own there. It is convinced that in this life the true 'Wisdom of Youth' will also be discovered.

But there is another opinion among the Youth. There are some who are tempted to take 'Youth' in so absolute a sense that even the striving for an esoteric life seems to them like the absorption of a foreign body. They want to be undisturbed by anything that comes to them from outside, so that they may penetrate their own full youthfulness and understand it. We may take it that the section who hold this opinion also hope to find something in the Anthroposophical Society, for otherwise they would not be in it. But they imagine that they must first give Anthroposophy its real spirit by bringing their own youth into play. The Executive of the Anthroposophical Society will be far from meeting them with pedantic criticisms. But it might easily happen that our own intentions appeared in such a light to some of the young folk themselves. For we cannot depart from the perception we have gained, namely that in the esoteric life which the Anthroposophical Society is attempting, that stream of Eternity for which Youth itself is striving, flows. We cannot fall into the error of supposing that the esoteric life must first receive its true form through the youthfulness of Youth. For we know that in the Esoteric the Youth themselves will find their true paths —paths which enable them to be young in the real sense.

I say this, not because I wish to indicate a contradiction between a certain section of the Youth and the Executive. I see no such contradiction; and indeed no such thing can exist for a practical view of the world. The Executive is aware that its tasks come to it from the spiritual world, and in all things it will have to take those paths which are pointed out to it from thence. In the sphere of its activity it can see no contradiction to this.

But it might happen that the Youth themselves would be driven into contradictions if the one section one-sidedly laid stress on their desires against the other. This would mean untold harm for the anthroposophical Youth Movement. It will not happen if the Youth will only beware of something which they have learned from this all too aged civilisation—I mean a certain proneness to abstraction, to speaking in mere abstract concepts. I said in the last number how ill this habit of abstraction goes with Youth. In reality no one in the Youth Movement wants it, but it is none the less there in their speeches about Youthfulness, about the ideals of Youth and so forth. There is indeed a baneful portion of old age in the Youth of today. If on the other hand the Youth will be mindful of their own true experiences, they will find that these are on every hand like questionings, to which the esoteric life of the Anthroposophical Society brings at any rate attempted answers. On the basis of such practical insight, an understanding between the several sections of opinion in our Youth Movement will certainly arise.

The very contact with esoteric life can become a living experience to the Youth. When this happens, the Youth will see that by this living contact they can realise the ideals which they so often place before themselves in a vague and undefined way. But if this were not to happen, it might easily turn out that some among the Youth cut themselves off from the living experience by a curtain of theory woven of old-sounding speeches—not indeed inborn—but picked up from the world around them.

If the Youth will understand themselves, they will understand the Executive of the Anthroposophical Society.

THE 'HUMAN ELEMENT' IN THE
SCHOOL OF SPIRITUAL SCIENCE

XII

THIS Institution cannot be founded on abstract considerations 'from above'. It must originate out of the needs of our own members 'from below'. The Executive of the Anthroposophical Society has planned to form a Section for the Youth, because this is to accord with what, in the depths of their hearts, the young people in our Society are seeking. And it will so shape this Section that these needs will be met to the degree in which they appear.

This will also apply to the other Sections. To this end it will be necessary that the needs which make themselves felt among our members should also really flow through the whole Society and finally unite in what is expected from the Executive at the Goetheanum. For this reason it should be realised more and more that the purpose of the Christmas Meeting was not merely to form an 'Executive Committee'. Such a Committee must of course exist. It should not be forgotten that an Executive is necessary and that it has to execute care and accuracy; but the chief thing will be, that through the attitude of the members the Executive at the Goetheanum is really placed at the centre of the spiritual interests of the Society. To it all these spiritual interests should flow.

It should be far remote from this Executive to limit initiative in any way in any direction in the various parts of the Society; but it should more and more be felt necessary to bring to the knowledge of the Executive all that arises in the Society. It can then harmonise what is wished in one place or by a certain group of people with what is desired in another quarter. This Executive will not wish to work in a one-sided manner like a kind of magistracy 'from above'; it will make it its task to have an open heart and an understanding mind for all that the members strive to achieve. On the other hand it would also like to be able to count upon being understood, by being met half-way, met actively, when out of its own initiative, out of the aims of the Anthroposophical Movement, it wishes to carry out something. In this sense I said at the Christmas gathering: The Executive Committee is to be a Committee of Initiative.

If the Executive is looked upon in this way more and more, it can in the right manner become the counsellor in all the affairs of the Society. And it would like to be a counsellor; for well it knows that it would fundamentally contradict the spirit of the Anthroposophical Society were it to wish to be an arranger. It will appeal with its advice to nothing else than the free insight of the members; but it will also become a real 'counsellor', if that which lies in the aims and efforts of the members is brought into its place in the right mood.

The Executive at the Goetheanum desires to establish a connection with the working in the Society as little as possible in paragraphs and programmes; it desires that the direct human element which can work individually even in detail, should come to quite general validity within the Society. And it desires above all to achieve in all its activities what really ought to be achieved for the development of the School of Spiritual Science.

EXTRACT FROM THE OPENING LECTURE OF THE COURSE GIVEN BY DR. STEINER IN BRESLAU ON 'KARMA AS THE WORKING OF DESTINY IN HUMAN LIFE'

SINCE the Christmas Foundation Meeting, Anthroposophical Movement and Anthroposophical Society have become identical, so that it must now be said: Formerly there was the anthroposophical teaching as cultivated through the Anthroposophical Movement; since the Christmas Foundation Meeting the Anthroposophical Society, by virtue of what it then became, has itself become an anthroposophical, nay actually an esoteric, reality. Since the Christmas Foundation Meeting our conception of the Anthroposophical Society must be that within it Anthroposophy is not only taught but that everything that is *done* is Anthroposophy. Since the Christmas Meeting, anthroposophical 'doing' is no longer separable from the Anthroposophical Society.

It is for this task that the esoteric Executive of the Anthroposophical Society at the Goetheanum, of which there are one or two representatives here, has been formed. It has been formed for the purpose of leading over anthroposophical teaching into anthroposophical 'doing'—in every detail. This anthroposophical-esoteric Executive will not be an administrative Committee but a Committee of initiative, giving the impulse for what should flow through the Anthroposophical Society as living reality. Naturally this can only happen slowly and by degrees. But after all, a fair amount has already been done through the members' News Sheet and through endeavours that have been made to give positive impulses of the kind that should proceed from the esoteric Executive.

Very little has been accomplished yet, but here again one should not attempt to take the fifth step before the third; it must be realised that things can only be done gradually. More and more initiative will be necessary, but what matters most of all is that people shall understand in what respects our administration must differ from all other kinds of administration in the world. It must be kept as free as possible from bureaucracy of any kind, basing itself entirely on the *human* element. The human relationships that should be woven between soul and soul within the Anthroposophical Society must constitute the reality by which the Society is quickened and furthered.

This human element can be brought to expression in small and in great things alike. Let me speak of just one trifle in order to show you what I mean. In order to give emphasis to certain matters connected with the Christmas Foundation, it was necessary to replace all the membership cards by new ones. There were 12,000 of these cards to sign. Many people advised me to use a stamp for these 12,000 signatures but I could not agree to such a proposal because a world-conception in keeping with reality knows that there is a difference when every card bearing the name of a member has been before me, when my eyes have rested for a moment upon the name and I have written my own by hand underneath it. This is a very slender relationship but it *is* a personal one. These personal relationships between soul and soul must be cultivated with ever-increasing intensity. People must understand that with us it is not a matter of sending out pronouncements into the world or of trying to reach this or that individual member; the point with us is always to stress *the human reality*. Naturally this will take time. This new trend which came into the Anthroposophical Society at the Christmas Foundation Meeting must be thoroughly grasped and understood. But it may also be said that the spiritual life which should flow through the Anthroposophical Society will contain an impulse leading more and more deeply into esotericism. And perhaps during these meetings when I can be among you, I shall be able in some small measure to convince you that this new impulse is a reality.

A NOTE FROM RUDOLF STEINER PRESS

We are an independent publisher and registered charity (non-profit organisation) dedicated to making available the work of Rudolf Steiner in English translation. We care a great deal about the content of our books and have hundreds of titles available – as printed books, ebooks and in audio formats.

As a publisher devoted to anthroposophy…

- We continually commission translations of previously unpublished works by Rudolf Steiner and invest in re-translating, editing and improving our editions.

- We are committed to making anthroposophy available to all by publishing introductory books as well as contemporary research.

- Our new print editions and ebooks are carefully checked and proofread for accuracy, and converted into all formats for all platforms.

- Our translations are officially authorised by Rudolf Steiner's estate in Dornach, Switzerland, to whom we pay royalties on sales, thus assisting their critical work.

look out for Rudolf Steiner Press as a mark of quality
ipport us today by buying our books, or contact us should
to sponsor specific titles or to support the charity
with a gift or legacy.

ce@rudolfsteinerpress.com
list at www.rudolfsteinerpress.com

JDOLF STEINER PRESS